Simple Rules

for...
The Road Warrior Princess!

*"Thee" Women's Inspirational Guide
To Embracing The Open Road!!!*

Debbie Anderson

Disclaimer: *The author assumes no liability for any incidental, consequential or other liability from the use of this information. All risks and damages, incidental or otherwise, arising from the use or misuse of the information contained herein are entirely the responsibility of the user. Although careful precaution has been taken in the preparation of this material and this publication is designed to provide competent and reliable information regarding the subject matter covered, the author and company specifically disclaim any liability that is incurred from the use or application of the contents of this book and assume no responsibility for omissions or errors.*

"Simple Rules for...The Road Warrior Princess" *is an independent informative entertainment product for consumers. The company and the author are not affiliated with, sponsored by or endorsed by any of the listed products or services in this book. Trademarks, service marks, logos, and or domain names (including without limitation, the individual names of products, services, companies, organizations, or retailers) are the property of their respective owners.*

Copyright © 2004, 2009 by Debbie D. Anderson
All Rights Reserved. No part of this book may be reproduced in any form or by any electronic or mechanical means, including information storage and or retrieval systems, without permission in writing from the author, except by a reviewer who may quote *brief* passages in a published review.

"Simple Rules" "Simple Rules for...The Road Warrior Princess" "Road Warrior Princess" "Simple Survival Kit" and "'Thee' Women's Inspirational Guide To Embracing The Open Road" are trademarks of Eminence Enterprises, LLC.

Published in association with Eminence Enterprises, LLC.

This book is sold subject to the condition that it shall not, by way of trade or otherwise, be lent, re-sold, hired out, or otherwise circulated without the author's prior consent in any form of binding or cover or by any electronic or mechanical means, including information storage and or retrieval systems, other than that in which it is published and without a similar condition including this condition being imposed on the subsequent purchaser.

If you purchase this book without a cover you should be aware that this book may have been stolen property. In such case, the author has not received any payment for this "stripped book".

Dedicated to my family, friends, and those who have inspired me throughout my great many journeys. Without your love and support, this book would not have been possible. Thank you!

A Word from the Author

First, I'd like to thank you for buying this book. In a crazy complex world such as ours, sometimes Simple Rules are not so simple to come by. After reading this book, I hope that you will feel more confident to take on the Open Road, to explore new horizons, and to free yourself in ways you've never felt possible before - because this isn't just a book about women learning to travel safely; this is a book about women taking on their own innate desires to explore the world alone – and to do it with safety in mind!

Growing up, I was always the adventuresome type. Before I could drive, I was a Bicycle Road Warrior. It was not uncommon to hear my mother yelling my name in the great outdoors because I had pedaled my way into yet another *lone starred adventure* beyond the trees and the mountain ranges of Idaho where I grew up. Going on a lone star adventure is more than just experiencing new and exciting things, *it is a test of will*. A journey to find out about one's self!

Upon reaching my 18th birthday, I took on my first truly great adventure in a car alone. I drove from Idaho to California by myself. I remember how terrified my friends, family members, employer, and everybody in my small hometown were for my safety, as well as how crazy they all thought I was for going down to California all by myself without already having a predetermined travel agenda. I hadn't planned a trip to go see anybody in particular. My only goal was to leave on a certain date and return on a certain date, two weeks later. Whatever happened in between these two dates was *my* Road Warrior Adventure!

Since that first road trip down to California as a young adult, I have enjoyed many Road Warrior Adventures around the United States,

Canada, and Mexico. From the Badlands of South Dakota to the Bright Lights of New York City to the Surf of Huntington Beach to the Big Horn Mountains of Wyoming to the Blue Ridge Mountains of Tennessee. These have all been my adventures, and I have learned *much* from these experiences. Not only about myself on a spiritual level, but about how to survive and rely on myself in even the most uncertain of circumstances, such as when I had to plow snow with my front car bumper for nearly 20 hours straight through during a massive nationwide blizzard or driving smack dab through windy tornado conditions in Ohio – Now there's a test of willpower and survival skills in a car!

I think it is important to say that these road trips are not just vacations; these road trips are about you, as a woman, creating a situation in which you have only yourself to rely on – a situation that will test your will to survive and your strengths as a human being. It is about giving yourself permission to embark upon a situation that will test your ability to guide yourself through this life safely – and most important, to test your ability to know yourself and to become your own best friend along the way. Road trips are as much about a spiritual *soul searching* experience and *soul growing* adventure as they are about the beautiful sites and the interesting people you will encounter as you take on the adventures of the Open Road.

For over a decade I have been regularly going on these Kamikaze Die-hard Road Warrior Adventures across the country, and it wasn't until driving through Wisconsin, when returning from my 10th cross-country adventure, that it dawned on me, I've learned a lot of useful skills, tips, tricks, and safety rules for traveling the Open Road alone as a woman.

Now most women get scared of traveling by themselves, and this I can completely understand. If you've never had to take on the Open Road by yourself before, it can be a little intimidating at first, but it's like going skydiving, so long as you know you have a parachute on your back, you feel just fine about jumping out of that plane! So consider this book your parachute and let yourself soar! There is a lot of beauty in this world and it would be a shame to miss it just because you didn't know how to dare it safely.

. . . . .

Contents

Dedication... **iii**

A Word from the Author... **v**

First and Foremost – Why Women Don't Become Road Warriors... **xi**

Rule #1 – A Road Warrior Princess Knows Her Vehicle BEFORE She Hits the Open Road... 1

    Non-Negotiable Road Warrior Vehicle Features... **4**

    Basic Car Items Every Woman Should Carry in Her Car – *and* Know How to Use Them... **7**

    Survival Road Warrior Tools... **9**

    Special Road Warrior Items... **11**

    The Simple Survival Kit... **14**

    Know Your Car Like You Know Your Own Body... **21**

    General Car Maintenance Every Woman Should Know... **23**

    Standard Timelines to Check Your Vehicle *Before* Your Journey... **35**

    Who Says the Everyday Woman Doesn't Know as Much as a Mechanic... **38**

Standard Timelines to Check Your Vehicle *During* Your Journey... **39**

Rule #2 – Packing Your Car is Half the Battle to a Successful Journey... 43

Never Look Like a Tourist by Keeping the Inside of Your Car (Relatively) Clean... **45**

What to Keep *Near You* While Driving... **46**

What to Keep *On You* "Just In Case"... **49**

Rule #3 – Don't Ever Let Other People Intimidate You... 51

Rule #4 – Tips, Tricks, and Very Solid Advice About Spending the Night Alone During Your Road Warrior Adventures... 55

The Truth About Rest Areas – 8 Simple Guidelines for Safety... **57**

The Truth About "Mini-Hotels"... **67**

The Truth About Gas Stations at Night... **69**

Rule #5 – The Truth About Where the Safest Gas Stations are Located... 71

Rule #6 – How to Get More Bang for Your Buck at the Pump... 75

Properly Maintaining Your Car is Half the Battle... **77**

The *Way You Drive* is the Other Half of the Battle... **79**

Rule #7 - In Case Of Emergency – Don't Panic! A Road Warrior Princess is Always Prepared... 97

What To Do If You Run Out of Fuel... **99**

What To Do If Your Car Starts To Overheat… **101**

What To Do If You Get a Flat Tire… **105**

What To Do If…It is Slick or Snowy Outside…or You Slide Into a Ditch…and Cannot Get Enough Traction to Get Going Again… **108**

What To Do If You Hear Your Car Making a Weird Noise While Driving… **109**

Rule #8 – The Truth About Truck Drivers and Large Trucks… 113

Lessons I Learned from My Dad About Sharing the Open Road with Truckers… **115**

Rule #9 – Maintain a Zen-like State of Mind Behind the Wheel… 119

Zen 101 for the Road Warrior Princess - Four Great Techniques to Get You Through Those "Not So Sure" Driving Situations… **121**

Maintain a Zen-like State of Mind Technique #1… **121**

Maintain a Zen-like State of Mind Technique #2… **123**

Maintain a Zen-like State of Mind Technique #3… **126**

Maintain a Zen-like State of Mind Technique #4… **128**

Rule #10 – Long Drives - How Does a Road Warrior Princess Keep Herself Awake… 131

Keeping Awake Solution #1… **133**

Keeping Awake Solution #2… **134**

Keeping Awake Solution #3… **134**

Rule #11 - The Journey – Knowing the Path is Like Knowing Yourself... 135

    The Inspiration... **137**

    The Challenge... **138**

    Fears Addressed... **139**

    Fear of the "What-ifs"... **139**

    Fear #1 – *"What-if"* I'm Not Brave, Courageous, or Adventuresome Enough to Take a Road Trip by Myself... **139**

    Fear #2 – *"What-if"* I Don't Have Enough Money... **143**

    Fear #3 – *"What-if"* Nobody Will Come With Me... **148**

    Fear #4 – *"What-if"* I Get Lost... **149**

    Fear #5 – *"What-if"* Something Happens... **151**

    Fear #6 – *"What-if"* I Have Kids? What Am I Suppose to Do With Them? I Can't Leave... **155**

    Fear #7 – *"What-if"* I Can't Leave My Job for *Too* Long... **157**

Closing Words... **159**

Quick Guide Index... **161**

First and Foremost –
Why Women Don't Become Road Warriors

The funny thing is, much like life, when you're on a road trip, you never truly know where you're going until you get there…and even then, you may wonder if you wound up in the right spot. The good news is, wherever you end up, there you are! Be confident that you ARE okay no matter where your journeys take you.

Over the years, and with a great many inspiring conversations under my belt, I've come to realize that sometimes, even in our most trying of moments, the one thing we, as individual beings, must always remember is: Rule Number One in Life; "You, as an individual, ARE important!" Much like special cargo that is being transported from Point A to Point B across the Atlantic Ocean or bullion transported by security trucks; when a Road Warrior Princess decides to embark upon a *lone star adventure*, she too has now become that very special cargo that must be cared for while embarking upon her journey. Thus, I would like to take this opportunity to pass along these words of wisdom to you. When you are driving alone on the road and you find yourself in a scary situation, just repeat these simple words to yourself, "I am carrying very special cargo, and I must deliver it to its destination safe."

Although this message is inspired by a series of self-help conversations I've had with others over the years that were focused more on the topic of traveling a spiritual journey in life than they were about going on an actual road trip, you'd be surprised at how convincing and effective the simple act of repeating these very simple words in your head can become when you find yourself trapped in a blizzard, driving through a small tornado, or just plain driving by yourself at night down a winding mountain highway that has WAY TOO MANY DEER grazing along the side of the road.

It is important to address the most obvious reason for why we as women do not venture out alone as often as our male counterparts – and the answer is clearly that we get scared about the "what-ifs?" Which is why, the first challenge in becoming a Road Warrior Princess is to nip your fears and "what-ifs" right in the bud. Repeat after me, "I am carrying very special cargo and I must deliver it to its destination safe!"

The best part about repeating this positive affirmation to yourself to overcome the "what-ifs" plaguing your every thought, is that it empowers you so that your destination can become anywhere – From the tops of the Rockies to the Jersey Shore – your destination as a Road Warrior Princess can be ANYWHERE your heart guides you to go. How many times have you wanted to just jump in your car and drive away? Many, I'm sure, but we, as women, tend to hold ourselves back. We don't *just jump in the car and drive away* because we are afraid that what is outside of our communities and familiar surroundings is so much scarier than just settling for the trivial madness we find ourselves surrounded by at home.

The Road Warrior Princess has confidence in her own abilities to not only take on the Open Road, but to know when she needs to go – to find her peace of mind – to find her new experiences – to find her inner voice – to find *herself* out on the Open Road – to determine her own destination – to listen to her intuition – and to know she is safe and held in high regard regardless of where the road might take her. The Road Warrior Princess knows that she is okay and safe, no matter what, which is why she has no problems with just jumping in her car and driving away for a day or two or a week or a month. The Road Warrior Princess is a survivor and a seeker of truth about herself.

So, be confident, be strong, take on the adventures of your heart's desires, and know that you as a Road Warrior Princess are never alone on the road. You *can* have faith in your own unique abilities, and this book, to guide you.

Simple Rule 1

A Road Warrior Princess

Knows Her Vehicle BEFORE

She Hits The Open Road!

Rule #1 – A Road Warrior Princess Knows Her Vehicle BEFORE She Hits the Open Road

This is not to say that you need to be a master mechanic or be willing to throw off those pumps to crawl under the car in order to be a Great Road Warrior Princess! This is just simple advice that will help you build confidence in your own ability to stay safe and ensure your enjoyment of the Open Road Experience.

First, most people ask me what kind of car they should buy. My simple answer is the least expensive "quality" car you can get with lots of horsepower and great gas mileage. The True Road Warrior Princess knows that buying the best value is always imperative, no matter what she does in life. Personally, I love my Sporty Lil' Economy Cars! They're great cars, plenty of room, killer gas mileage (I've done 50+ miles to the gallon when the winds were pushing behind me), and the upper end models have a lot of torque at the bottom (in other words, I can take off fast from a dead stop). These cars also provide enough horsepower to pass a slow moving truck going up a long steep mountain climb, such as in the Rockies (elevation over 6,000 feet above sea level at the Continental Divide marker on I-90 in Montana). *Plus*, speaking from a few mishap experiences when I unknowingly locked my keys in the front seat of my car, these cars are also impossibly difficult to break into with an auto lockout tool – Having this knowledge about one's car is very important when you're braving unfamiliar territory alone.

Regardless of the Road Warrior Vehicle you decide upon, the following is a list of non-negotiable features to consider when looking for the Perfect Road Warrior Vehicle for your many adventures:

Non-Negotiable Road Warrior Vehicle Features

Good Gas Mileage *without Sacrificing Horsepower* – Let's face it, as of the writing of this book, the gas pumps haven't exactly been giving us a discount on the price of gas in the United States these past few years – so shop with this in mind and what you don't spend on gas you can spend on having FUN!

Anti-lock Brakes – You need to have control when you hit those brakes!

Full Frontal Airbags and Seat Belts – Truth vs. Fiction - There *are* maniac drivers out there and these are just some good features to have in working order on any Road Warrior Vehicle!

Lots of Torque on the Low End of the Transmission – When you need to get out of the way of some crazy person, you need the transmission and "horses under the hood" working together to ensure you *move at the exact moment* you hit the gas pedal *telling* your car to move!

Plenty of Horsepower Under the Hood – Test drive your car and see if you still have more power to speed up quickly, even when you're already traveling at high speeds, such as 65 or 75 miles an hour. This is important because when you hit those open plains, such as in Montana – it seems like everybody drives 80 or 90 miles an hour out there. Make sure your car has enough "horses under the hood" to get you out of harm's way should you ever need to, even at high speeds and when driving up steep inclines.

Air Conditioning – This is critical during a rainstorm or when driving in areas that are typically pretty humid (think of weather conditions on nearly the entire Eastern Half of the United States). Not only can it defog windows in a pinch, Air Conditioning also works as a gentle cooling system, which can come in handy during those blazing hot days on the California I-5.

We will discuss later in this book how this feature is used for different driving safety techniques and driving situations, but for now, just know that having a strong Air Conditioning unit and fan on your car is a non-negotiable – You must have it to stay safe when exploring the Open Road!

A Good Heater with Front, Side, and Rear Window Defrost Features – In contrast to the Air Conditioner, try driving through South Dakota in the dead of winter with a wind chill factor of -50 degrees Fahrenheit weather conditions working against you? A powerful heating unit with a strong heater fan is a MUST for the Road Warrior Princess.

Fog Lights – The Road Warrior Princess MUST SEE where she is going, day, or night, in ANY type of weather – make sure you have these!

Automatic Side View Mirrors – Auto adjustable side view mirrors that can be adjusted from inside the driver's side of the car is a non-negotiable feature because of the way I will teach you to use them for your safety and protection when stopping in a rest area (or whenever you need to pull off the road to get some shuteye).

A CD Player or MP3 Compatible Player/Stereo with AM/FM and/or HD Radio Receiver Capabilities – Truthfully, if you're doing a 10,000-mile road trip over the course of one month, as I have, you can't possibly stand entertaining yourself with ONLY your own thoughts for all 10,000 miles. Get a Car Stereo System *with buttons that are easy to navigate **without** having to look at the Control Panel or Face Plate every time you want to change the song* (we'll talk more about this later in the book).

A Good Radio Antenna – If you can't listen to the Road Advisory Stations you don't know what is happening further up the road…and that, my friend, is how you suddenly find yourself driving smack dab into the center of a tornado! Enough said - Make sure your car has a good Radio Antenna!

Cup Holders – Test out the cup holders in your car to make sure that they actually restrict the movement of a bottle of water or your favorite size cup of fountain soda. I know this doesn't sound like it's crucial to your safety on the road, but surprisingly, it is! Example: **IF** you're worried about spilling your drink every time you wind around a curve in the road or make a sharp turn around a city corner, **THEN** you are not paying attention to the road (you're watching your drink). Make sure you have good factory Cup Holders in your car, and if your car doesn't have this feature, you can usually pick up an inexpensive Console Attachment for your Road Warrior Vehicle that comes equipped with plenty of appropriately sized Cup Holders at your local auto parts store or at your local mega "one stop shopping" superstore.

A Power Source Plug - (Formerly known as the "Car Cigarette Lighter") – A power source plug in the front console area within easy reach of the driver's seat is a critical feature during a Road Warrior Princess' journeys. After all, cell phones are our best friends – and when you're a Road Warrior Princess – Your cell phone *is your very best friend* (aside from your car of course)! So having a good place to plug it in is essential. Whether you want to surf the internet on your laptop to look for new attractions along the way or you want to call a friend to see if they have watched the weather report for your present area of the nation, you must keep these things charged up in order for them to do you any good. A great example is if your cell phone is running low on battery power while you're puttering through Chicago traffic at 4:30 in the afternoon, you will want to have your cell phone plugged in and charging *while* you're talking on the phone with your friend *without* having to suddenly take your eyes off the road just to plug it in. (Besides, you may just get the chance to creep 2 feet forward in that heavy traffic and you don't want to miss out on *that* great opportunity all because you're fiddling around with power cords!)

Large Trunk Space – This isn't to say that you need to buy the biggest luxury car on the market, just make sure you have plenty of trunk space (you will understand why as we further discuss the rest of the Simple Rules for the Road Warrior Princess to keep you safe during your travels).

Collapsible Rear Seats – A "non-negotiable feature" for one reason - if you need to get into the trunk of your car to get something out (oh say, a toothbrush?) at 3:00 in the morning, why should you have to get out of your nice warm car and expose all of your personal belongings in the trunk of your car to the entire world? Furthermore, what if this happens to be in the dead of winter? Say in the mountains of Wyoming? You don't want to get out of your car and freeze your toosh off anyway! Make sure your Road Warrior Vehicle is fully equipped with a convenient Collapsible Rear Seat arrangement and you'll thank me for it later!

These features pretty much sum up the non-negotiable factory car features for the Road Warrior Princess. These features are not luxuries; they are survival tools for the Open Road! Spend the money to have these simple features on your car and feel confident that you are well on your way to breaking free as a Woman of the Open Road!

Basic Car Items Every Woman Should Carry in Her Car – *and* Know How to Use Them

As a Rule – You're only stranded if you aren't prepared to deal with whatever comes your way. The Road Warrior Princess is Always Prepared!

First of all, it drives me insane that women do not have the following item in their cars. As a matter of fact, it appalls me that society as a whole doesn't encourage women to carry this one thing in their cars, at all times. So, because I care about you and your safety as a fellow Road Warrior Princess, I am going to clue you in right now – BUY A TOOL KIT FOR YOUR CAR!!!

This is the most important, and most commonly overlooked, item for women with cars. Even if you never go on a road trip completely by yourself – place a multifunctional tool kit in your car and leave it there. This item is as critical to you and your car's well-being as carrying a spare tire in your car (commonly referred to as a "Donut"). It doesn't cost a lot of money and you'll feel empowered for having taken care of yourself and your vehicle so intelligently.

When shopping for a multifunctional tool kit, which can be purchased for very little money online or at any home improvement store, mega "one stop shopping" superstore, or any other local retail store that sells mechanical tools, you should make sure *your* Tool Kit includes the following tools:

A Screwdriver – Most tool kits have Ratchet or Multifunctional Screwdrivers where all you have to do is insert the appropriate bit on the end of the shaft, and "voila!" now you can unscrew or screw in any size screw with any type of screw head pattern that your car might have holding it together. If the tool kit you purchase *does not* have a Multifunctional Screwdriver, make sure you have at least One Flat Head Screwdriver, the tip looks like a straight line (-), and at least One Phillips Head Screwdriver, where the tip looks like a small cross or plus sign (+).

Pliers and Long Nose Pliers – Do not be mistaken, not all pliers are the same. The traditional pair of pliers offered in most tool kits are great to have in *your* tool kit, but if you don't have a pair of LONG NOSE PLIERS in there too, then you've kind of defeated yourself. Long Nose Pliers typically have wire cutters built into them so you can take the sleeve (the plastic covering) off of a wire, should you ever need to use them for this purpose. More important, Long Nose Pliers also come in handy for reaching little things that have been dropped into small or tight spaces, pulling on a hood lever cable if the plastic handle breaks off in the dead of winter (yes, I'm speaking from experience, remember that –50 degrees weather in South Dakota I mentioned earlier?), and many other useful purposes.

A Ratchet with Metric and Standard Size Sockets – This is entirely necessary when looking under the hood. Sometimes there is a screw holding things together, but usually it's a bolt of some sort. Be prepared for both.

Wrenches – Both Metric and Standard Sizes – As I said before, sometimes there is a screw holding things together and sometimes there is a bolt with a nut attached to the other end of it. You need to be prepared no matter what is holding the parts of your Road Warrior Vehicle together. Metric Wrenches are measured in millimeters and Standard Wrenches are based on inches. More than likely, you have a mix of both of these types of bolts and nuts on your car. Be prepared to use both.

A Razor Blade – Sometimes you have to cut things, even if it's just opening a package of light bulbs or fuses for your car. It's always a good idea to have one of these handy.

A Roll of Black Electrical Tape – Now why in the world would you plan on having *this* in your car unless you plan on playing with the wiring in your car? The good news is, it's multifunctional! If you have to change a light bulb in your taillight and you notice a wire connection has pulled loose from another wire that *it should be* connected with, you can tie the two wires together (make sure they actually go together) and then wrap a small strip of Black Electrical Tape around the connecting wires to prevent water from dripping on the wires and shorting out the connection. Or, if your windshield wiper comes loose mid-adventure, wrap a little bit of this around the windshield wiper blade and the windshield wiper bracket so you can at least get to the next gas station or auto parts store safely (Duct Tape also works wonders in this scenario).

A Hammer – Now why would you need a Hammer in your car? You'd be surprised at the unlimited number of circumstances that come up, but the fact is, sometimes you need a tool to help you put a little muscle into things. Keep a Hammer in *Your* Tool Kit!

Survival Road Warrior Tools

Beyond the Basic Car Tool Kit, the following are a few other items every Road Warrior Princess should keep in her car *at all times*:

A Flashlight with Extra Batteries – Also, periodically check that you always have enough extra *fresh* batteries in the car that are the correct size for your flashlight.

Car Tire Air Pressure Gauge - Put it in your vehicle's glove box and leave it in there!

One Quart of Oil and Oil Funnel – The next time you get your oil changed, ask the service center technician to sell you an extra quart of the same brand and weight oil that they just put in your car. Leave this Extra Quart of Oil in the trunk or storage area near the spare tire in your car and while you're purchasing preparation items, you may also want to consider purchasing a small Oil Funnel to keep in the car as well. This way you won't have to worry about spilling oil all over the engine block, should you ever need to add oil to your engine at a moment's notice during your road trip. With this little bit of preparation, you'll be thankful you have this item handy in your car because spilled oil on the engine block can create a horrendous smell, not to mention blue smoke as it burns, while driving down the road if you accidentally leak too much oil while adding it to the engine.

In addition to storing Extra Oil and an Oil Funnel in your car, if you do not know where to check the oil level in your car (commonly referred to as the "Dipstick") or where to refill the oil in your car, ask one of the mechanics changing your oil to show you how to check the oil in your car's engine and where to add more oil should you need to do this while braving the Open Road.

Jumper Cables – or BETTER – There are now power pack systems that have the jumper cables attached to them called **Jump Start Kits**. Jump Start Kits are the best invention known to women because you can "jump-start" your car all by yourself without ever having to approach a stranger for help with getting your car started. Batteries can go dead for all sorts of reasons. Some of my favorite reasons are draining the battery down by leaving your lights on, listening to the radio all night without turning on the engine periodically to recharge your car battery (yep, I'm guilty!), or freezing cold weather can also unsuspectingly drain the life out of your car battery in the dead of winter.

You can usually purchase Jumper Cables or a Jump Start Kit online, at any auto parts store, or at your local mega "one stop shopping" superstore.

Road Flares – It's just a good idea.

A Bottle or a Quart of Water – It's multifunctional. If you're driving through the deserts of Nevada and Arizona in July, both you and your car's radiator just might be happy that you thought in advance to put this in the trunk of your car.

Windshield Washer Fluid – This is a *must have* that we rarely ever think about until it's too late. When you're driving down the Open Road, you rarely have a clue as to how many bugs might hit your window - how muddy the rain will be in a given area of the country (harvest time?) - or get forewarning about whether you will be driving through a blizzard one minute and then driving in –50 degrees weather where the bitter cold frost builds up on your windshield like a block of ice the next minute. For this very reason, it is always a great idea to keep *extra* Windshield Washer Fluid in the trunk of your car for just these types of extreme driving situations during your journey!

A Note About Windshield Washer Fluids

***Road Warrior Tip:* Not All Windshield Washer Fluids are Created Equal!** If you are driving from a warm climate to a cold climate, please make sure you carry Windshield Washer Fluid that has Antifreeze in it in your car. Yes, you can use water or other Windshield Washer Fluids that do not have Antifreeze in them, BUT! There is nothing worse than going from the warm sandy beaches of Florida to two days later driving through a blizzard and your Windshield Washer Fluid Sprayers are suddenly frozen over because the Windshield Washer Fluid you put in your car is frozen as solid as a rock under the hood. Know where you're going during what time of year and use the appropriate fluids.

Road Atlas with Spiral Binding – Even if you have a Global Positioning System (GPS) unit for your Road Warrior Vehicle – ALWAYS have one of these handy inside your car! The best ones usually have maps for each state in the United States, each province in Canada, an overall bird's-eye view map of the United States (so you can draw a line all the way across the country if necessary), and additional road maps that are far more specific and detailed for most major cities in the U.S. and Canada. Even better, many also have maps for most Major International Airports. It's some of the best money you'll ever spend!

Special Road Warrior Items

This leads us to *Special Items* you should ALWAYS KEEP IN YOUR CAR if you are going on a long road trip by yourself because we have all heard stories about people, both male and female, being stranded on the side of the road in some remote unpopulated area and by the time they are found, or help arrives, some or all of the people are found dead.

    Specifically, one story comes to mind when I was on a road trip driving through the deserts of Nevada with my family as a young child.

There was nothing out there in those days, and I remember seeing two bodies lying on the hood of a broken down car with a big blue tarp lying over the bodies one morning as we drove down the road. I asked my dad what happened to them. His response was that the car probably "broke down" and since it was almost 300 miles to the next town, the people in the car must have overheated and died of sunstroke or something. He further speculated that an officer must have found them during a patrol of the area, but had to cover them up with a tarp in order to drive close enough to the next town to radio for help. The severity of the impression that experience made on me has always stayed with me when I travel alone because these types of stories are the very stories that create our fears for not wanting to travel alone – especially as women.

Thankfully, the following items can potentially help ensure your safety - should something horrendous happen to you while going down the road (Example: Your Road Warrior Vehicle decides to breakdown in the middle of the afternoon under a blazing hot sun). These Special Items are very simple items and when it comes to taking a Road Warrior Adventure lasting longer than 3 hours - *I NEVER TRAVEL WITHOUT THEM!*

Road Warrior Tip: The following Special Items are most useful when kept *inside your car*, near the driver's seat of the car when possible. A few suggested places to store these items are in the Glove Box (next to this book), in the storage space provided in the Center Armrest Console, or in the side storage slot on the inside of your car doors, if you have space to put things there.

Special Road Warrior Items

A Multipurpose Tool – These tools are lifesavers! They oftentimes come with Pliers, a Knife, a Can Opener, a Bottle Opener, a File, Scissors, a Flat Head and/or a Phillips Head Screwdriver, sometimes Tweezers, etc.. Personally, I love my Gerber Multipurpose Tool that neatly stores away in the inside pocket of my driver's side door because *this one item has managed to save me* from so many strange and sometimes dangerous situations while traveling that aside from my car purchase, I truly consider this one item some of the best money I ever spent!

Road Warrior Story - I say my Gerber Tool is some of the best money I ever spent because, just to name one example, one time I was driving through South Dakota in the dead of winter during one of my notorious East Coast to West Coast Cross-Country Adventures and the piece of metal covering my gas cap (that is suppose to flip open when I pull the little lever inside the car) had frozen itself shut and would not budge open in the chilling sub-zero South Dakota winter weather. I remember it was *brittle* cold that day and I was completely out of gas by the time I'd found a town to refuel because I'd missed the turnoff for the last gas station 30 miles back. The thing is, there wasn't another gas station for another 100 miles at this point, and since I was in a little town, inconveniently located in the middle of nowhere, where there really wasn't *anybody* nearby except for the gas station attendant lady, and even then, I was wondering where in the world she came from, my options were definitely limited at this point. I could either figure out a way to get gas in my car, or freeze in my car. Needless to say, I opted for option number one, pulled out my Gerber, and pried the gas cover open so I could put gas in the car. Then, I thanked myself for being so well prepared and continued on my journey through the winter wonderland of the North.

The key to preparation and *carrying these Special Items inside your car*, is that, such as in this instance, I didn't have to dig through my trunk to find the tools I needed to pry open the gas flap cover, because the trunk was also frozen shut from the ice that had built up on the outside of the car; I just had to grab my Gerber out of the inside pocket on the driver's side door in order to overcome the obstacle standing between my filling up my tank with gas or winding up stranded in sub-zero weather. Thankfully, *all it took* was a Multipurpose Hand Tool to overcome this obstacle so I could fill up the fuel tank and become free to get back to my Road Warrior Adventure!

So my advice to all Road Warrior Princesses everywhere, "Keep a Multipurpose Tool *inside your car*!" This one act of Road Warrior Preparation alone could very well prevent a bad situation from ever becoming an even far worse situation, had you not been prepared.

A Multipurpose Emergency Car Escape Tool – This is a tool that is designed to help you break free from your Road Warrior Vehicle should you be involved in a serious automobile accident. This is an All-In-One Hand Tool that typically comes equipped with a Flashlight, a Protected Razor Edge for cutting seat belts, a Sharp Point or Dulled Hammer on one end for breaking glass, such as a driver's side window, and a Retractable Poker that pushes up for popping an airbag that could potentially decide not to deflate after the initial impact during a car accident. Keep this tool *easily within arm's reach* of your comfortable driving position, because if you *are* in an accident and need this tool, you will need to be able to reach it fast and know how to use it quickly!

Emergency Medical Kit – Prepare or purchase a small Emergency Medical Kit with Bandages, Clippers, Tweezers, a Sewing Kit for making stitches, Gauze Wrap, Medical Tape, Antiseptic, Bug Repellant, etc. because something will always happen where you need at least one bandage, and if it's already in the car, you're already taken care of!

A Blanket or a "Quillow" – As women, we love having tons of quilts and throw blankets around the house, but very few of us think to carry one in our cars at all times. The way I see it, the fact that you haven't any idea *when* you might need a throw blanket of some type in your car, just indicates that you *will* need one at some point. Some blankets are huge, and that's entirely unnecessary for a car. I use what is called a "Quillow", and it's great! A Quillow is essentially a blanket or quilt that folds up into a small pocket sewn into one side of the blanket, and once folded up, it then becomes a pillow! Not only are Quillows super warm, they are also easily stored in the trunk of your Road Warrior Vehicle or under the driver's seat too! To have this super cool bit of comfort on your next Road Warrior Adventure, you can make your own Quillow, purchase one online, or inquire at your local arts and crafts store to find out if anybody in your home town knows how to make one for you!

The Simple Survival Kit

- **One or Two 30-Gallon Clear Plastic Garbage Bags** – Similar to what you would use for collecting yard leaves or throwing out recyclables.
- **A One-Gallon Plastic Bag** - Such as a zipper or self-sealing plastic bag.
- **1-2 Thick Rubber Bands**

- **A Condom *without* Lubricant** – Not for what you might think!
- **A Small Metal Cup** - Bring more cups with you if you are traveling with children or other people.
- **1-2 Books of Matches, *or* a Flint Lighter**
- **Napkins** – The next time you go through a fast food drive-thru, just leave the extra napkins in the car.
- **A Roll of Toilet Paper** – You'd be surprised at how often you will need this!
- **2-3 Packages of Instant Chicken Noodle Soup**
- **2-3 Individually Wrapped Tea Bags**
- **2-3 Individually Wrapped Single Serving Packages of Hot Cocoa Mix**
- **2-3 Individually Wrapped Single Serving Packages of Crackers**

* Store *ALL* Simple Survival Kit Items Neatly *INSIDE* the One-Gallon Plastic Bag.

Now why keep such funny things *inside* your car? It's not as though you are going camping – You're going on a ROAD TRIP, right? Well, what happens if you hit a deer and nobody finds you until the next morning stranded on the side of the road? Better yet, what if it's cold outside and you can't turn your car engine on to warm up during the night?

The Simple Survival Kit - Protect Yourself From Hypothermia!

The 30-Gallon Garbage Bag is meant for you to sleep inside of it in the event that you can't turn on your car's engine to use the heater for keeping warm at night. This will keep your body heat circulating inside the bag so you are less likely to get hypothermia. If you're short like me, one bag should be fine, if you're really tall, keep a couple of these bags in your car. Whether you're using one bag or two bags, always remember that your head needs to be outside of the plastic bag, not inside of the bag, while you are resting! If you're tall and need to use a second garbage bag to cover the upper half of your body, simply use the knife on your multipurpose tool to slice an opening in the bottom of the second large bag so you have enough room for your head to pop through the hole, and then pull the rest of the bag down around the torso of your body until the bottom of the bag meets the top of the bag that is pulled up and over the lower half of your body. These bags can also be used to create a temporary shelter to protect you from the wind in the event you ever wind up having to spend the night outside of your car due to an endless list of circumstances that can occur during your journey.

The reason for a *Metal* Cup is because *IF* you have to keep warm outside of your car, or you cannot turn on your car's heater to keep you warm, you still need to keep yourself warm. Using the Book of Matches or Lighter and Dry Napkins or Toilet Paper inside your Simple Survival Kit start a small fire (outside of your car) and try to find dried shrubs, small sticks, and other sources of fuel to keep the fire burning. Place the Metal Cup from your Simple Survival Kit in the hottest area of the fire to heat up water and use the hot water to make Instant Chicken Noodle Soup, Tea, or Hot Cocoa (as found in your Simple Survival Kit) to stay warm until help arrives.

Alternatively, if *you are stranded **and** you can still turn on your car's engine **and** you are able to keep the motor running for at least 15-20 minutes* - In the absence of being able to build a small fire outside of your car, another method for heating up bottled water or melting snow or ice for drinking water is by placing the Metal Cup, with the water, snow, or ice inside the cup, on the engine block while the engine is running.

Caution: Before using this method to heat up water for soup, tea, or cocoa, or before using the heat from the engine block to melt and boil snow or ice for drinking water, make sure you are aware of, and take precautions to avoid, any possible engine fluid leaks that could potentially contaminate the water inside your Metal Cup.

The Simple Survival Kit – Keep Your Energy Up!

Should you become stranded and you are all out of soup, cocoa, and tea to keep your belly feeling warm and full, as a last resort to starvation and to curb the hunger pains, the Crackers in your Simple Survival Kit can be rationed over a period of time so you don't starve while waiting for help to arrive. Snack Bars and Protein Bars are also a good choice to store in your Simple Survival Kit; however, Individually Wrapped Packages of Crackers (such as the ones served with soups at restaurants) can usually be acquired at little extra cost to you, so this is an added bonus for the *Budget Conscious* Road Warrior Princess!

The Simple Survival Kit - Never Go Thirsty!

The One-Gallon Plastic Bag, Rubber Bands, and Metal Cups are in your Simple Survival Kit for making your own water, should you ever need to do this during your Road Warrior Adventures. These items are especially important if your car breaks down in the middle of the desert during a heat wave.

    Now, if you have ever looked inside your refrigerator and noticed that the containers you have covered in plastic wrap are now building condensation on the inside lining of the plastic wrap, this is the exact same concept we are going to use to create drinking water under the hot desert sun. Although there are many alternative ways to create drinking water when stranded in the desert, we are going to discuss two techniques for producing water in the barren desert based on the Solar Still concept. One technique utilizes a plant leaf or a plant root as a water source and the second technique utilizes water that is already stored in the soil to create drinking water. Neither one of these survival techniques are intended to replace quality forms of drinking water, and when possible, you should always try to filter out any large particles or plant life in the water created, as well as, boil the water first before drinking it. However, if you find yourself in ***dire circumstances***, the following two survival tips may help save your life when stranded beneath the blazing sun:

The Simple Survival Kit – Hydration Techniques One and Two

Lending tribute to a few tips, tricks, and good solid advice I picked up along the way from back in the day when I was involved with Civil Air Patrol Search and Rescue as a youngster, the following hydration survival techniques in this chapter are variations on a concept known as a Solar Still that generally functions under the principles of the "greenhouse effect".

Among those in the "survival" world, the Solar Still has been attributed to being created by two engineers working for the United States Department of Agriculture as a survival tool and has allowed for many to find new ways to survive in the wilderness when there is no fresh drinking water nearby.

The process behind how this survival tip works, is that when solar energy (the sun) heats the ground or a large water source, by passing through a clear plastic barrier, the moisture from the water source, such as soil or a plant leaf or a plant root, then evaporates, rises into the air, and by our creating a barrier with the plastic so that this water condenses on the underside of the plastic barrier above the cup, we have now trapped this condensation and can use a rock or a pebble to redirect the moisture back into our Metal Drinking Cup to create a new water source for hydration!

The Simple Survival Kit - Hydration Technique One

Place a Small Plant Leaf or a Plant Root inside the Metal Drinking Cup and wrap the One-Gallon Plastic Baggy around the outside of the cup. Next, place the Rubber Band around the outside perimeter of the cup's edges to seal the edges of the plastic bag around the edges of the cup so that the plastic bag is securely in place. Find a Small Round Rock or a Small Pebble and place it in the center of the plastic bag that is covering the opening at the top of the metal cup. The pressure from the rock or pebble will create a 45-degree angled slope in the plastic and create a "dripping point" for the condensation that builds up on the inside of the plastic covering of the cup to flow toward. Place the cup directly in the sun and let the condensation buildup on the underside of the plastic so that it drips down into the inside of the cup.

A Word of Warning: The upside of using this technique is that you will have at least some water to stay hydrated. The downside is that you need to be especially careful about the "type" of plant you use as your water source so that you are not drinking water from a poisonous plant. After all, this method assumes you only have One Metal Cup, One Small Plastic Bag, and One or Two Rubber Bands to create drinking water (and that there is some form of vegetation nearby).

Alternatively, if you have a Bowl or a Container that is deeper and wider than your cup, place the plant leaves or roots in the larger container and then set the metal cup inside the center of the larger container with the plastic bag securely sealed off around the larger container. This will allow your drinking water to remain cleaner than if you have to dig a plant root or plant leaves out of your cup before drinking the water!

The Simple Survival Kit - Hydration Technique Two

Find an area in the soil or sand where there is a depression in the soil. Depressions in the soil could possibly mean that these depressions are areas in the soil where rainwater could have possibly collected during the last rainstorm or where a previous water hole may have been formed at some point. The soil or sand should be soft and easy to dig in that area. Next, use your hands, a shovel, a walking stick, or anything you can find to dig a hole that is approximately 3-4 feet wide by 2-3 feet deep. In the center of the hole, dig a smaller hole that is large enough for your Metal Cup and place the Metal Cup with the opening facing up toward the top of the hole. Use the knife on your Multipurpose Tool to cut your 30-Gallon Plastic Garbage Bag in half (so that it is one long strip of plastic) and lay the plastic over the hole so that the ends of the plastic are covering the entire width of the hole's opening. Anchor the edges of the plastic on the ground's surface with rocks, then place a Small Round Pebble or a Light Weight Rock in the center of the plastic above the metal cup inside the hole so that the plastic cover over the hole is sloping down toward the center of the hole (and the cup) at a 45-degree angle. Finally, secure the entire perimeter of the plastic with rocks and dirt so that the plastic DOES NOT fall into the hole you have just dug. Usually, within an hour or two of sunlight, the cup should begin filling up with condensation (water) from the underside of the plastic.

Additionally, if by some small miracle you have a Long Rubber Tube or Hose that you can place inside the cup and then guide the other end of the tube outside of the hole so that the tube runs out from underneath the plastic before covering the hole with your plastic garbage bag - This additional item will allow you to drink water from the metal cup without having to remove the plastic covering over the hole in order to drink the water!

The Simple Survival Kit – Hydration Technique Three

Last but not least, I'm sure you were curious about the Non-Lubricated Condom and how this fits into the Simple Survival Kit's safety plan! Should you find a natural source for drinking water while stranded, when it comes to carrying a gallon of water, a condom will do this job just as easily as a large bulky plastic container can. However, the condom is a little more compact and discrete to store during your Road Warrior Adventures! Besides, why have a bulky plastic jug in your car that is taking up the space where a new pair of shoes could fit, when you can put a Non-Lubricated Condom in your Simple Survival Kit and have the Non-Lubricated Condom serve the same purpose as a One-Gallon Plastic Jug? And if you store an XL Non-Lubricated Condom in your Simple Survival Kit, this size condom has been known to hold up to SEVEN GALLONS of water before breaking! With THIS MUCH water stored away in a condom while stranded, you could stay hydrated for up to a week or more while waiting for help to arrive!

The Simple Survival Kit – Hydration Technique Four

Alternatively, if you don't feel like digging a hole in the ground or hunting around for plant leaves and roots that are safe for you to drink the water from them, nor do you feel like breaking out your condom for mere hydration survival purposes under not–so-great circumstances; the least complicated way to rehydrate under the desert sun is to just pull out that bottle or quart of water you were advised to always leave in the trunk of your car and enjoy the scenery until help arrives!

The Simple Survival Kit Overview

From the 30-Gallon Clear Garbage Bag to the Individually Wrapped Single Serving Packages of Crackers, all of these survival items in your Simple Survival Kit *will fit* nicely inside your self-sealing One-Gallon Plastic Bag and *could* end up saving your life one day. Shove it under the driver or passenger's side seat of your car if you must, but ALWAYS keep this little Simple Survival Kit in your Road Warrior Vehicle whenever you are embarking upon the Great Adventures of the Road Warrior Princess!

Know Your Car Like You Know Your Own Body

On the Open Road, your car is an extension of your own body. It is your baby with four tires, a steering wheel, and a bunch of horses under the hood that are as much a part of you, as you are of it. In order to be safe and prepared for any situation on the road, as a Great Road Warrior Princess should be, you *must know your car like you know your own body.*

So what does this mean?

Knowing your own car like you know your own body means that you don't have to look at your hand to know which finger you have just touched with your other hand – assuming of course that you haven't suffered any nerve damage – the point being, that you need to know where everything is located in and on your car without having to physically look at it if this is what the road requires of you at a specific moment in time. This is particularly important when we are talking about the controls in the front cockpit of your car (including your CD Player, MP3 Player, and the AM/FM or Satellite Radio for your Car Stereo).

I know it sounds kind of silly to advise you to sit in your stationary car in the driveway and practice playing with each of your vehicle's controls without looking at each of them before reaching for them, but it is good advice. Not to mention, to truly be prepared for your great many adventures, this one exercise alone, of practicing and learning where each of your controls are located in the cockpit of your Road Warrior Vehicle without having to look at them each time you reach for them, can REALLY help prepare you to efficiently handle most any driving situation or driving condition you might encounter while out on the Open Road.

I can't tell you how many times I've suddenly driven into a blinding storm where my windows fogged up so thick and so fast that it looked like somebody just placed a piece of cardboard over my windows. The worst part about driving situations like this on the road, is that usually only seconds after this happens, I've always known that the last time I was able to see anything before I was suddenly blinded by an unanticipated storm (typically only seconds beforehand), I knew there had been at least a half a dozen other cars near *my car* on the freeway. Many times, these situations have happened when I have driven into a rain or snowstorm that was so fierce and so heavy that I suddenly couldn't see so much as even 5 feet in front of me, with other vehicles right beside me, behind me, or in front of me.

Road Warrior Story - The scariest of these situations was a time when I was driving down a two-way highway and shortly after my windows became "blinders" by the fierce storm, my only thoughts revolved around the fact that I knew the last thing I saw before becoming blinded was that there was a car in the oncoming lane speeding toward me and I could no longer see it! Now that's a scary situation!

These types of situations create those moments in life when you hear about a 10, 20, or 40 car pileup on the freeway during the evening news report, and you think to yourself, "Dear God! How did that happen? What would have caused such a tragedy?" The answer is, in many circumstances, people didn't know how to watch the road, and adjust their vehicle's controls, simultaneously. They couldn't adjust the controls on their vehicle to adjust for the situation at hand fast enough because they had to *physically look* at their vehicle's controls in order to adjust them, thus taking their eyes off the road, and then they couldn't focus back to what was happening on the road quick enough in order to avoid danger. It is the "little adjustments" that need to be made when every millisecond matters. It is the fact that these drivers possibly couldn't turn on the Air Conditioner and Windshield Defrost Fan almost simultaneously (one of the fastest ways to reduce condensation, or "fog buildup", on the inside of your car windows during a rainstorm, especially in humid areas of the country), or they couldn't turn on the Windshield Wipers or the Car Lights - FAST ENOUGH - without taking their eyes off the road and this is when tragedy struck their vehicle.

YOU MUST KNOW YOUR CAR LIKE YOU KNOW YOUR OWN BODY (If you are to become a *Safe* Road Warrior Princess)!

So *practice, practice, practice,* and do whatever steps are necessary for you to know your car like you know your own body. I can't stress this enough because it is so critical to you and your car's survival when partaking in the beauty and adventures of cruising the Open Road alone!

General Car Maintenance Every Woman Should Know

Unfortunately, we live in a society where most women are thought of as not knowing much, if anything, about cars and because of this stereotype, we don't. This is a *generally accepted perception about women* that I feel should change. Now, I'm not telling you to throw off that skirt and crawl under your car wearing a pair of mechanic's overalls, but I do think you should understand the basics of taking care of your own vehicle because not every place you travel will be kind to your wallet by doing it for you.

"MAX" and "MIN" Road Warrior Vehicle Fluid Lines – Most of the time, the "MAX" Fluid Line is typically marked just a little below the very top of the container holding the fluid. Do Not Fill Fluids Above the "MAX" Fluid Line – this little bit of space between the "MAX" Line and the bottom of the lid on the container holding the fluid is necessary for your car to work properly. Additionally, never allow your car's various fluid levels to fall below the "MIN" Fluid Line marked on each container under the hood of your Road Warrior Vehicle. Not having *enough* of any one particular auto fluid can also prevent your vehicle from working properly.

Checking the Oil in Your Car's Engine - If you don't know where the Dipstick is located under the hood of your car – do yourself a favor and pull out your car manufacturer's auto manual and look at the pictures to figure it out. This knowledge can be a "road trip saver" as you're embracing the freedoms of embarking upon the Open Road alone!

As when checking any of your car's fluids, always TURN OFF your Road Warrior Vehicle's engine *before* pulling out the dipstick to check your oil levels. Once you locate the dipstick and pull it straight up and out of your car's engine, note that there are typically two little grooves on the end of the dipstick that are about an inch or so apart from each other (located on the end of the dipstick furthest away from the handle). Your oil should reach up toward the notch furthest away from the tip of the dipstick (usually located about 1 ½ inches up the rod from the end of the dipstick's metal rod tip – this is the "MAX" Line). If the oil is closer to the notch that is closest to the tip at the end of the dipstick (usually about a ¼ inch from the tip – this is the "MIN" Line) then it's time to add a little more oil to your vehicle.

Adding Oil to Your Car's Engine - This really isn't as scary as it sounds, even if you have never done it before. To add more oil to your car, place the dipstick back in the engine block where you pulled it out of originally, locate the cap that says Engine Oil or Oil (refer to your car manual for exact location), and unscrew the cap. Open the quart of engine oil that is stored in the trunk of your car and add about half a quart of engine oil to your engine, at first. Wait about 15 seconds after you stop pouring oil into the engine and then pull the dipstick back out. Check to see if the oil is now closer to the second notch that is located furthest away from the tip of the dipstick. If the oil is above the notch *closest* to the tip of the dipstick, you should be okay. If it is not, add more oil.

Road Warrior Tip: *If you have added an entire quart of oil and the thin film of oil creeping up the dipstick still doesn't creep up **above** the lower notch on the dipstick,* use a clean rag to wipe off the dipstick, and then check the engine oil level one more time using a clean dipstick.

If using a clean rag to wipe off the dipstick before checking the levels still doesn't change what you see as your oil level on the dipstick, put the dipstick back in the engine block and screw the engine oil cap back onto the engine block tightly (make sure it's on there tight). Start up your car and allow the engine to run for approximately 30 seconds. After the engine has run for about 30 seconds, turn off your car's engine and check the dipstick again to see if the oil is now closer to the "MAX" Line (the second notch on the dipstick) and confirm that there isn't any oil moving up the rod of the dipstick toward the handle beyond the second notch.

If you still don't notice a change on the dipstick, make sure you are parked on an even and level ground surface. If your car *is* parked on a slanted ground surface while checking the oil levels in your car, the unlevel surface that the car is parked on can cause the reading on the dipstick to become inaccurate. Make sure your Road Warrior Vehicle is parked on a level surface and check the oil levels in your car again.

When All Else Fails: If you continue having a problem with adding enough oil to your engine so it will register on the dipstick properly, (assuming your oil light isn't on or the engine hasn't seized up) drive your car to the nearest oil change service center because there *could be* a more serious issue going on with your car's engine than the General Car Maintenance topics covered in this book.

Checking and Adding Windshield Wiper (Washer) Fluid - Under the front hood of your car and usually toward the front of your engine (please refer to your car's user manual for exact location) you will see what is usually a clear-ish or white plastic tube-like container with a blue cap on it (usually it's a blue cap). The blue cap usually has a raised or embossed symbol of a "windshield" or a "windshield wiper" on it. This is your Windshield Wiper Fluid Holder. Lift up on the cap to pop the cap off and look inside the container. If you can't see any windshield wiper fluid, pour more into it. Fill the tube up with windshield wiper fluid until just about an inch or two from the top of the container. Push the cap down to snap the lid back into place on the container and then jiggle the cap "just a little bit" to make sure that the cap is back on the container "snug and tight".

Road Warrior Tip: If you are adding windshield wiper fluid to your car in exceptionally cold or winter weather, make sure you are using windshield wiper fluid that says it has antifreeze already added to it on the front of the bottle label. Do NOT add your own antifreeze to the bottle of windshield wiper fluid yourself if the label on your bottle does NOT say that it already has antifreeze added in the bottle! The "better to be safe than sorry" approach might be to just purchase a new bottle of windshield wiper fluid *with* antifreeze clearly stated on the outside bottle label, and this way your fluid sprayers won't freeze up while driving through freezing cold weather or while you're enjoying the scenic, and yet sometimes scary experience, of driving through a heavy snowstorm on the freeway. Besides, you can always use the bottle of windshield wiper fluid *without* the antifreeze already added to it to scrape the bugs off your window while going down the road during your Road Warrior Adventures in the summer months!

Checking and Filling Up the Coolant (Antifreeze) *for* Your Car's Radiator – *NEVER Add Coolant "IN" Your Car's Radiator*

A Word of Warning: I don't care what you've seen in the movies! Do NOT take the cap off of the radiator – EVER!!! Even if your car *has been* sitting without the engine running for a few hours, the liquid inside the radiator is still scolding hot (yes, even in winter) and it is also *highly* pressurized – so if you remove the cap on the radiator – you will most likely get burned!

The second reason to NEVER remove the cap on the radiator yourself is because you can seriously damage your radiator by removing the cap and releasing all of the pressure that needs to remain *inside* your radiator. This is why we will focus on using the Radiator's Coolant Reserve Container to check coolant (also called antifreeze) levels and for adding coolant to your Road Warrior Vehicle!

After turning off your Road Warrior Vehicle's engine, look under the hood of the car and locate the radiator's coolant reserve container. This container is usually located next to the radiator near the front of your car's engine. As you look under the hood, you will see a square plastic container (usually it's a square or rectangle shape) with greenish-yellow liquid inside of it. The container is typically located just to the right or just to the left of the actual radiator with a hose running out of the container and into the radiator (check your car's user manual for exact location on your car). This container near the actual car radiator is your radiator's coolant reserve container. It is OKAY to take the cap off of the RADIATOR'S COOLANT RESERVE CONTAINER – just NOT the RADIATOR!

Looking at the side of the container, you will notice two level lines marked on the container. The line on the bottom of the container will say "MIN" and the line about 3-4 inches above the "MIN" Line says "MAX". The liquid level in this plastic container should be somewhere in between these two lines. If it is not, and the coolant or antifreeze (terms commonly used interchangeably) is below the "MIN" Line, you can do the following:

You should purchase coolant, also called antifreeze, and pour it directly into the radiator's COOLANT RESERVE CONTAINER ONLY – DO NOT pour this liquid directly into the radiator (or you can get seriously hurt, injured, or worse)! Next, fill the radiator's coolant reserve container up to the "MAX" Line with coolant or antifreeze, but never over the "MAX" Line, or this could create a problem while driving. Finally, screw the lid back onto the radiator's coolant reserve container and you're back on the road!

**Caution:* Make sure that the lid is screwed back onto the radiator's coolant reserve container properly or the lid could come off while you're driving and the coolant can spray out of the container causing the car to overheat and eventually seize up the engine – so, make sure the cap is back on "good n' tight"!

Alternatively...

If it is hot outside and you are not at a location where you can purchase antifreeze (coolant) for your car, you can also pour water into the radiator's coolant reserve container until the liquid just reaches the "MAX" Line, but never over the "MAX" Line or this could create an engine problem while driving – especially when climbing steep hills or driving up long winding grades.

Should you not have enough water to fill the container all the way up to the "MAX" line, so long as you can fill up the container until the liquid level reaches at least to, or above, the "MIN" Fluid Line, you should be okay until you can add more coolant or water at the next service station.

Road Warrior Tip Number One: *Overheating on a Hot Day with NO Coolant* - If you notice that your car is overheating while driving up a steep grade and you suspect this is happening because your coolant is below the "MIN" Line in your radiator's coolant reserve container – And, if you find yourself on the verge of being stranded on the side of the road and all you have in the car is a small bottle of your Favorite Name Brand Water, but it isn't very much - Use the water to try and get the radiator's coolant reserve level back up to the "MIN" Line, just until you can safely arrive at the nearest gas station or auto supply store where you can then fill it all the way back up to the "MAX" Line with coolant or antifreeze.

Road Warrior Tip Number Two: *Adding Antifreeze (or Coolant) to Your Radiator's Coolant Reserve Container During Freezing Cold Weather* **-** If it is winter or cold outside, please find someplace that sells *antifreeze* (usually any gas station). Unfortunately, pouring *water* in the radiator's coolant reserve container during freezing cold weather can possibly freeze up once in your cooling system and essentially end your road trip.

Checking Your Steering Fluid - Anymore, just about every car has power steering, but for those of you with an old '57 Chevy (or similar older model cars), you can skip this section and jump forward to the next section in this book.

For those of you that DO have power steering, after referring to your car's user manual for the exact location under the hood to check this fluid, unscrew the cap where the steering fluid container is located to check that the liquid level is between the "MIN" and "MAX" Lines. If it is, just make sure the cap is on tight and you're good to go!

If the steering fluid is below the "MIN" Line – refer to your car's user manual for the exact type of steering fluid recommended for your particular vehicle; go to the nearest gas station or auto parts store that sells car fluids; and purchase a bottle of the recommended steering fluid for your particular Road Warrior Vehicle. Remove the cap where the steering fluid *should be added* to your vehicle and fill the container up to the "MAX" Line. After adding more steering fluid, make sure the cap (under the hood of your car) is back on tight and you're good to go!

Checking Your Brake Fluid - Please refer to your car's user manual for the exact location under your hood. Check to make sure the liquid level is between the "MIN" and "MAX" Lines. If it is, just make sure the cap is on tight and you're good to go!

If it is below the "MIN" Line – refer to your manual for the exact type of brake fluid recommended for your car, go to the nearest gas station or auto parts store that sells car fluids, and pick up a bottle. Remove the cap and fill to the "MAX" Line, then make sure the cap is back on tight and you're good to go!

Checking Your Transmission Fluid - Please refer to your car's user manual for the exact location under your hood. Check to make sure the liquid level is between the "MIN" and "MAX" Lines. If it is, just make sure the cap is on tight and you're good to go!

If it is below the "MIN" Line – refer to your car's user manual for the exact type of transmission fluid recommended for your car, go to the nearest gas station or auto parts store that sells car fluids, and pick up a bottle. Remove the cap and fill to the "MAX" Line, then make sure the cap is back on tight and you're good to go!

Checking the Air Pressure in Your Tires – Quick vs. Thorough

The Quick Check

As a general rule, it is recommended that you always check your Road Warrior Vehicle's tires for proper air pressure whenever you get in your car to drive it, but we don't really do that – do we? We usually only notice we have a low or flat tire *after* we get in the car and start driving down the road. Or, when we are met with the sudden and unwelcomed realization that we no longer have the same amount of control over our steering the way we once did.

Now that we've stated the obvious about our lack of enthusiasm for checking tire pressure every day, a more practical rule of thumb is to always kick the tires to check for good air pressure every week or two, and ALWAYS CHECK YOUR TIRE AIR PRESSURE if there has been a sudden change in the weather temperature. When weather temperatures change dramatically, checking the tire pressure is critical to your safety, regardless of whether or not you are traveling long distances or are only driving around town to run a few errands. Tires tend to adjust in air pressure as the weather fluctuates from Hot to Cold and from Cold to Hot.

When Kicking the Tires

Notice if one tire seems to "give-in" a little more than the other tires do when you kick them, or if one tire looks a little "bulgier" on the bottom of the tire next to the ground than the other tires do. This tire could have a slow leak, or just need a little air added to it due to outside temperature changes. (If you fill it up and the same tire keeps losing air pressure, you could have a slow leak – take it to a tire service center and tell them you need it checked for a slow leak.)

Complete a Full Inspection of Your Tires' Air Pressure

First, know how many Pounds (of pressure) per Square Inch (psi) your tires need. This should be in your car's owner manual, embossed on the sidewalls of your tires, or it may also be on the invoice of the last service provider that changed your oil for you, that is, if they checked the tire pressure during the oil change. Get to know this number well (*know your car like you know your own body*) because this is the number you're striving for when you fill up the air in your tires.

Most gas stations offer free air, but a lot of them do not have an air gauge for you to use, so make sure you use the Tire Air Pressure Gauge from your glove box to ensure that the proper amount of air is in all four of your car's tires. ALL FOUR TIRES SHOULD ALWAYS HAVE THE SAME READING! – This Is Very Important!

To check the air pressure in your tires remove the Tire Valve Stem Cap on the Tire Valve Stem, and then push the indented portion of the tire air pressure gauge tightly against the top of the tire valve stem. Regardless of whether you buy the Standard $3.00 Tire Air Pressure Gauge or the $40 Electronic Tire Air Pressure Gauge, your tire air pressure gauge will give you a reading. For example, my tires need to be at 35 psi (pounds per square inch), so if my $3.00 tire gauge says that the pressure is between the 30 and 32 psi notches, it means I need to hold the air hose on the tire valve stem for another few seconds to put more air in the tires. After holding down the air hose on the tire valve stem for a few more seconds, I would check the tire with my tire air pressure gauge again. If it gives me a reading between the 34 and 36 psi marks on the tire air pressure gauge, then I know I'm pretty close to exactly 35 psi (pounds per square inch) in that tire. Repeat this procedure on all four tires until each tire reads the exact same psi reading for all four tires on your Road Warrior Vehicle.

What-if I Overinflate My Tires?

A common fear I hear many women mention is that airing up their tires scares them because "what-if" they overfill the tire with air and it blows up at them? This is a great question! Here's how to protect yourself from overfilling your tires with air:

Road Warrior Tip: On the sidewall of every tire on your car, located near the portion of your tire where the black rubber from the tire meets the metal or aluminum wheel frame, you will notice some letters and numbers raised in the tire rubber. If you look closely, you will see the words "## psi MAX." Every type of tire has a different number for the maximum psi that that particular tire can handle – So long as you never fill up your tires with air beyond the MAX psi number written on your tires (the MAX psi your tires can handle), you're generally safe while filling up your tires with air.

Road Warrior Story - On the sidewalls of my tires, each tire says, "44 psi MAX". When I look at this number, it tells me that I can only put a maximum air pressure of 44 psi in my tires or I risk causing harm to my tires, myself, and my car, because any amount of air pressure beyond 44 psi is considered, by the tire's manufacturer and test standards, to be *unsafe*.

Needless to say, I was extremely upset the time I had my oil changed at one of those "quick" oil change service stations and the guy checking my tires filled up each tire to 45 and 46 psi (remember, they only have a 44 psi MAX).

I was on one of my infamous cross-country road trips at the time and didn't realize what had happened until I was already 200 miles down the road. When I decided to check my tires because the car was suddenly driving "a little funny" (strange), not only were two of the tires overinflated beyond 44 psi, the other two tires on my car were nearly 10 psi below where I normally kept my tires (at 35 psi). Consequently, to fix this little service center mess up, I had to deflate two of the tires and inflate the other two to make sure that all four of my tires were back at 35 psi.

My Road Warrior Lesson that day was that it just goes to show, you really do need to double-check your technician's work after you get your car serviced!

The Best Solution for Fixing Overinflated Tires

Hold your tire air pressure gauge down on the tire valve stem for a few seconds. When doing this, you will notice that while the tire air pressure gauge is taking a reading of your tire pressure some of the air in the tire is also actually being let out of the tire so that the air pressure coming out of the tire can create the reading on the tire air pressure gauge. If the tire is far too full, just lightly hold the tire air pressure gauge down on the tire valve stem of the overinflated tire until you have released enough air pressure in the tire to bring the psi number back down to where you need it to be. Then, continue to add or release air pressure until your tire is finally reading the correct psi number for your tires on the tire air pressure gauge.

Changing Turn Signal Bulbs, Taillight Bulbs, and Burnt-out Headlights - About once a month, you should check your turn signal bulbs, taillight bulbs, and headlights (for both high-beams and low-beams) on the front and rear of the vehicle to make sure that they are working properly. Sometimes this is done for you if you go to an oil change service center that does a multiple point inspection of your car at the same time they are changing the oil. If your service center does not check the turn signal bulbs, taillight bulbs, and headlights for you, it really is a good idea to do it yourself with the help of a friend, family member, or neighbor.

If you do need to change a burnt-out headlight, for newer cars, the best course of action is to just take your vehicle into an auto parts service center to do it for you because of the way headlights are designed in newer cars. However, for vehicles in their 1970s and older, in my experience, these vehicles tend to be a bit more straightforward and generally only require the appropriate screwdriver bit to swap out the headlamp quickly. However, regardless of the age of your Road Warrior Vehicle, if you feel uncertain about swapping out a headlamp on your car yourself, always consult a professional mechanic.

Turn signal bulbs and taillight bulbs are a little easier to switch-out. To change a taillight bulb, it's as simple as opening up your trunk popping out the old light bulb and snapping in the new light bulb. Sometimes there will be a plate cover with a screw holding the cover in place over the turn signal or taillight bulbs; this is where your Car Tool Kit comes in handy! The cover is simple to remove and it is easy to replace these bulbs, so never fear, you can do it!

Changing Windshield Wipers - If your windshield wipers are squeaky, fraying, ripped, flopping in the wind as you drive down the road, or just flat out not doing their job anymore during a major rainstorm, then it's time to replace them. As a general rule, which is a rule that has been created after 8 cars worth of experience in this department, I have concluded that the only GOOD brand of windshield wiper for your car, is the car manufacturer's windshield wiper brand. This seems silly, but it's true. The Automobile's Factory Windshield Wiper Blades Always Seem To Work Best!

However, if you really do need to change your windshield wiper blades and you don't want to pay an arm and a leg for them (metaphorically speaking) at your car dealership's service center, go to the nearest auto parts store and ask them which type of windshield wiper blades your car takes and which Name Brand Windshield Wiper Blades they use on *their own* car or truck.

This last part of your inquiry will help give you a better idea about whether or not the person you are talking with actually has an opinion about which windshield wiper blades are best *and* that they *trust to use* on their own cars, *or* if they're just trying to sell you the most expensive ones in the store. Most newer vehicles require one longer wiper blade and one shorter wiper blade, so make sure you get the PARTS NUMBER for the windshield wiper blades that are designed *specifically* for the make, model, and sometimes even the engine type for *your* Road Warrior Vehicle! – I know the engine model doesn't seem like it would be all that important when purchasing new windshield wiper blades; however, when making any auto part purchase for your Road Warrior Vehicle at any auto parts store, all of this information is good to have handy because this detailed information is how many auto parts stores actually catalog the inventory in their systems – and you definitely want the correct parts for your car or truck! (Example: Is your vehicle the 4-cylinder engine model or the V6 engine model?)

To Replace Just the Windshield Wiper Blades - (Rubber Section Only)

There is a little clip on the far end of the bracket that usually looks like a little arrow (>). Squeeze the outer edges of the arrow together on the clip and slide the rubber strip (the wiper blade) out of the bracket. Slide the new wiper blade back into the bracket in the exact same direction that you pulled the old wiper blade out of the bracket. You will know the wiper blade is in its proper position when you feel the little arrow clip "click" and lock into position. Make sure it clicks or you could lose your wiper blade the second you turn on the windshield wipers!

To Replace the Windshield Wiper Brackets and the Blades

This really isn't all that more complicated. The entire bracket (usually) has a little plastic upside down "J" shaped attachment that pulls up and away from the windshield wiper arm. Lift it up and off of the windshield wiper arm and put the new one back on the windshield wiper arm in the exact same way that you took off the old bracket (only pushing in the opposite direction to lock it into place). It's that easy!

Checking and Changing Your Air Filter - First of all, you really shouldn't have to pay people to change this for you. It's ridiculously easy to check and to change your air filter, when necessary. Usually, when you start noticing that your car seems to cut out a bit when hitting the accelerator, it could be a sign that you need to check your air filter (also, do this more frequently if you live in areas of the country where there is a lot of humidity).

The air filter is usually positioned under a lid with clips that lock it into place (refer to your car's user manual for the exact location). To push the clips away and uncover the air filter, use the Flat Head Screwdriver from your car tool kit. Once the cover is removed, pull out the air filter and inspect it. If there is a lot of dirt, leaves, pine needles, or debris in there, blow off the air filter or brush it off with your hands, a clean towel, or a clean brush to get rid of the excess debris. Then, place the air filter back into the air filter holder the exact same way you originally pulled it out of the air filter holder. *IF* your current air filter looks as though more than 50% of the air filter is covered with "ground-in" dirt that can't be wiped away or blown off of the air filter, you should put the old air filter back in the air filter holder and put the cover back on. Then go to your local auto parts store, buy the air filter that is right for your car, and replace the old air filter with the new air filter.

Road Warrior Tip: The cover is very easy to lock back into place, just make sure that you hear the clips "snap" into place. That sound will tell you that the air filter cover has locked into place before driving anywhere.

This pretty much concludes basic car maintenance. All of these tasks are fairly straightforward and easy to perform, and now that you know how to do them, you'll be able to save a few dollars for your next road trip by doing it yourself.

Standard Timelines to Check Your Vehicle *Before* Your Journey

So now that you know what to check and how-to check it, the question is: How often should you check these things?

BEFORE You Leave for Your Road Trip, Make Sure You Complete the Following:

Scheduled Tune-ups - If there is a regularly scheduled maintenance check-up or tune-up for your car (e.g. the 60,000 or 80,000 mile tune-up) coming up, get it done *before* you even think of getting on the road.

Oil Changes - Make sure you get the oil changed and have all of the fluids and tires checked before hitting the Open Road - ***and*** remember to double check the fluid levels and tire pressure yourself after the service is performed because remember the technician that checked my tires during an oil change? Don't become a victim of careless car service center technicians!

Timing Belts - Make sure that if you are scheduled to get your timing belt changed in the next few thousand miles and you plan on going on a fairly extensive road trip – my advice is to just go-ahead and get that timing belt replaced (and cooling system looked over at the same time).

A Word About Timing Belts

If your timing belt breaks (for cars typically 60,000 miles or over, consult your car's user manual for the exact mileage requirements for *your* Road Warrior Vehicle) while you are on your Road Warrior Adventure, this can destroy your engine. *IF* your car's engine is near, at, or OVER the recommended mileage to receive a timing belt change, get the timing belt replaced (and have the cooling system done at the same time) BEFORE you go on your road trip. This is imperative! I once saw the dismantled engine parts from a car that *did* have the timing belt break while the owner of the car was driving down the road; let's just say it wasn't pretty, and it wasn't cheap to fix either (think thousands of dollars vs. the few hundred it would've cost to prevent the entire incident).

Suspension and Braking Systems - Have the brakes, shocks, struts, and rotors looked at if it seems like it has been a while (more than 6 months) since you had them inspected.

Road Warrior Tip: – Always know roughly how much you have left on your brakes (e.g. 50%, 20%, etc.), this way you never come by this knowledge accidentally (think "auto accident").

Tire Check - Have the tire tread checked on your tires. Are there any nails, screws, or shards of glass puncturing the tire tread? Do you still have a nice thick or fairly thick tread on your tires, or are they balding and you will need new tires before you hit the Open Road? Tires, although expensive, are essential to the Road Warrior Princess' safety. If you don't have tires that can grip the road, you can't go very far down the road – not safely, anyway. *Purchase good tires and you will buy peace of mind while traveling* – after all, you never know what kind of weather you will hit while embracing the Open Road, so be prepared for anything!

Road Warrior Story - During one of the last road trips I completed while driving cross-country, I drove through a slick rainstorm on Thursday, slick and windy tornado conditions on Friday, sunshine and dry roads on Saturday, and a blinding snow blizzard on Sunday. WOW! Gotta have good tires for that kind of a weekend!

Wheel Alignments – First, there are ALL WHEEL ALIGNMENTS, there are FRONT WHEEL ALIGNMENTS, and there are REAR WHEEL ALIGNMENTS (typically only done with a full-wheel alignment). Always know which type of alignment your tire service center is talking about performing on your vehicle before having the work done. No offense, but many mechanics still think that, as women, we know very little about this sort of thing. My advice: Always stay "in the know" about your car's maintenance and understand exactly *what* the mechanics working on the vehicle are doing to *your* Road

Warrior Vehicle in order to avoid unnecessary hassles and added maintenance or repair costs.

A Word About Wheel Alignments

My other piece of advice about getting an alignment done to your car, is to only get a wheel alignment (front or all wheel) done if you're noticing that it is becoming more difficult to steer your car, or if you notice that you are constantly having to pull harder to the left or right on the steering wheel in order to drive a straight line down an evenly paved and unobstructed road. Depending on where you live, you could need an alignment every 10,000 to 15,000 miles or you could need one after you finally reach 100,000 miles. Have your alignment checked more often if you live, or frequently drive, in an area where there are a lot of potholes, rough, or poorly maintained roads, otherwise ask your tire service center technician about it the next time you have new tires put on your car.

Road Warrior Tip: Once you get an All Wheel or Front Wheel Alignment performed on your Road Warrior Vehicle, double check the alignment job completed on your vehicle by driving down a long straight and evenly paved stretch of road (or a large vacant parking lot is sometimes a safer place to do this test) at moderate speeds. Once you are driving in a straight line, briefly let go of the steering wheel to see how the steering on the car is doing. If after removing your hands from the steering wheel the car no longer continues driving in a straight line, then the tire service center didn't adjust your wheel alignment properly and you will need to go back to have them correct their work. Make sure you get this done right away, as driving with poor alignment can create unnecessary wear and tear on your vehicle and can also create for dangerous driving situations on the road. Also, do not feel bad about taking your car back to the service center to have them fix the problem, as all too often women are shy about doing this. The reality is; it's your money that just paid for their mistake so make sure *your money* was well spent by taking it back and having the job done right! After all, YOUR safety out on the Open Road IS worth the return trip to the tire service center!

Who Says the Everyday Woman Doesn't Know as Much as a Mechanic?

Since we're talking about taking our cars to the service center and having to deal with sometimes-rude mechanics, I think this would be a good time to address the pathetic manner in which, not all, but some, mechanics treat women who bring their cars in to receive check-ups, tune-ups, and general maintenance service for their vehicles. First of all, as a community of women, we are not incompetent about our cars, and I think it's time the car service industry acknowledges this fact about women! I have heard about so many of my female friends, family members, and business associates getting ripped off because they're told by some "mechanic" that they needed to replace car parts that had nothing wrong with them, that I can't possible tolerate this senseless mentality anymore - and to be honest, I'm tired of women getting ripped off at the "Car Service Center".

So, the next time you think you're being "taken for a ride" (figuratively speaking) by your mechanic ask him, or her, these simple questions: "Where is the damaged part? I want to take it home.", or "Show me how my part doesn't work and compare it to a working part by showing me on a new part (before they install it) how this particular part is suppose to work." This way you can see for yourself what is wrong with *your* vehicle's supposedly useless part and why it needs to be replaced so badly (according to the mechanic). If the mechanic really is trying to rip you off – they'll freeze up and tell you the work is possibly something that could, "probably wait for a while if you didn't want to do it today."

Unfortunately, a quick change in opinions, like this example, once the mechanic is challenged to explain his (or her) "sales pitch" to you is a strong indicator that you are on the verge of being ripped off. After all, if the work the mechanic claimed needed done is "definitely something that needs to be fixed today," *before* you asked for an explanation, only for their *professional opinion* to suddenly change into "It's something that can wait." *after* asking - there is a good chance that this change in responses was the mechanic's way of trying to get you to purchase parts and services that your Road Warrior Vehicle doesn't actually need! Don't let it happen to you! ASK GOOD QUESTIONS and stay "in the know" about your vehicle!

Better yet, if after challenging the mechanic to explain why you need this particular part or service done to your car "today" and you have asked to be shown how everything works, and the mechanic *does* have a good explanation and *has* shown you so that you can see for yourself *why* the part or service needs to be performed on your car "today", then by all means, have the work performed and consider yourself lucky to have now gained valuable knowledge about your Road Warrior Vehicle that will most certainly come in handy as you continue to embrace the Open Road alone during your Road Warrior Adventures!

Standard Timelines to Check Your Vehicle *During* Your Journey

Finally, the car checks out, you've got a full tank of fuel – You're all excited and you're ready to go! Hooray! You're on the road! Now are you really sure your car will be all right for however many thousands of miles you decide to go before you return home? Of course it will be, so long as you make sure to check things periodically while on the road.

First Rule of On-the-Road Road Warrior Maintenance - Always check your oil levels when you fuel up – or at least every other time you fuel up. You never know when something might have come loose near the oil pan, or if you have an older car engine, your engine could be burning a little oil because of age and use, or if you're climbing a lot of long steep grades and hills during your trip, these types of strenuous driving conditions on your car's engine can also cause your engine to burn a little extra oil. So just remember to check the oil every few hundred miles to make sure everything is okay. It only takes a minute or two and that is time well spent considering the alternative of being caught by surprise when your oil light unsuspectingly comes on or your engine seizes up while driving down the road because the engine is suddenly out of oil.

Second Rule of On-the-Road Road Warrior Maintenance - Since you're checking your oil anyway, why not glance at the other fluids and make sure that they all have some sort of liquid still sitting between the "MAX" and "MIN" Lines?

Third Rule of On-the-Road Road Warrior Maintenance - Make it a habit to kick the tires to check for proper air pressure *every time* you get out of your car to get gas or whenever you pull into a rest area. As you travel across different climates and different elevations, your tires will have a tendency to fluctuate in air pressure. Make sure you pull out your tire air pressure gauge and check the tires at a gas station where you can get some air, if necessary, every time you notice the weather temperature significantly changing between warmer or colder air outside, or when you are up in a high elevation, and then quickly travel to an area located closer to sea level or vice versa.

A Side Note About Tires

Always remember to periodically check your tires' tread (the part touching the road) to make sure you don't have any nails, screws, or pieces of glass puncturing the tires. It can be a *real bummer* if you do get a nail stuck in your tire while driving down the freeway (only the tire doesn't go flat, just yet) only to find that it suddenly decides to start deflating just as you hit a bump in the road.

Road Warrior Story - I had this happen to me one time in South Carolina. I noticed my tire wobbling (while driving 65 mph on the freeway) and by the time I could come to a complete stop at a gas station off the freeway, a nail my tire picked up from the road had already shredded my tire and the air blew right out the sidewall of the tire after stopping. I'm really happy that the tire didn't have a blowout *while* I was still driving down the freeway going 65 miles per hour, because that happening really would've killed my Road Warrior Adventure (and possibly me too)!

So, just make sure you check the tread on your tires every so often, and if you notice a problem, take time out of your fun adventure to immediately deal with the problem, get the tire patched up, or whatever it takes to repair it, so you can safely get back on the road again. When it comes to road trips – prevention works best!

Fourth Rule of On-the-Road Road Warrior Maintenance - If you are not going to be home to get your oil changed before completing 4,000 miles, just pull into a quickie oil change service center during your travels and get it done there. Fresh oil keeps your motor running better, and if it runs better, you get better fuel mileage *and* a better performance while you're cruising the Open Road! Plus! - You can usually watch the technicians as they check your tires, auto fluids, headlights, turn signals, and taillights for you too, so it's one less thing for you to do!

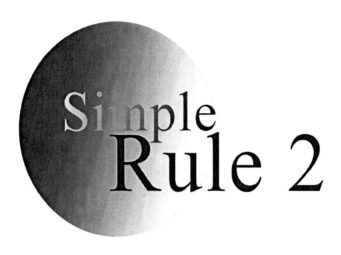

Simple Rule 2

Packing Your Car Is

Half The Battle

To A Successful Journey!

Rule #2 – Packing Your Car is Half the Battle to a Successful Journey

Never Look Like a Tourist by Keeping the Inside of Your Car (Relatively) Clean!

The fact is, as women, we love to pack ALL sorts of stuff when we go on an adventure, and as women, I think we should be able to do just that! It's our right!

HOWEVER! As a general rule to Road Warrior Princess Safety, keep in mind, the more "clutter" you have inside the car, the more it looks like you're traveling a long ways from home all by your little ol' lonesome! Not to mention, when you enter larger cities: Chicago, Los Angeles, New York, Detroit, Denver, Dallas, Philadelphia, etc., you don't want to have to worry about somebody breaking into your car because you have all sorts of cool looking items lying all over the inside of your vehicle.

Whatever items you are bringing with you on your trip should fit neatly inside your trunk, including changes of clothes, pillows, blankets, and anything of value that makes you look like a Die-hard Traveler or Tourist. This is why I have put "a large trunk space" on the list of non-negotiable factory car features when considering a new car purchase because it is for your own safety. If you pull into a rest area and your Road Warrior Vehicle looks more like the inside of a RV Motorhome than the inside of a car, somebody might just want to get a closer look once you get out of sight of your car. This is not good. "Never look like a tourist by keeping the inside of your car relatively clean!" This is a rule I have always followed and it has always kept me safe!

This Simple Rule *especially* includes, NEVER leaving your suitcase in the rear seat of your Road Warrior Vehicle (and if you *absolutely must* – then cover it up)! Otherwise, this is a surefire way to call attention to yourself. Keep the suitcase, or suitcases, in the trunk.

So what if you have a hatchback or SUV and you can't cover it up? Not a problem! Place it behind the rear seat and throw your blanket over it. For any readers out there who are a bit more "fashion conscious" about the interior of your cars, most manufacturers and auto parts stores also sell covers for the rear storage areas of hatchbacks and SUVs so that other people cannot see what you have stored behind the rear seat. The colors offered are usually black, gray, or tan to compliment the interior of your car and look great in the back of any vehicle!

Earlier in the book, I mentioned that fold down seats are a Critical Road Warrior Traveling Feature for your Road Warrior Vehicle. The reason this is a "non-negotiable" feature is because you don't want to leave your pillows, blankets, toothbrushes, and any items that you won't readily need while driving, out in the open. Since you will only need access to these items periodically throughout the road trip, these items should be placed to the far back of your trunk near the trunk's side of the collapsible rear seats. This way, all you have to do is drop down the rear seat in your car to grab your pillow, toothbrush, hairbrush, or any other necessary items from the comfort of being inside the car. The benefits of this feature are: 1) you can avoid freezing your toosh off during the winter months by not having to get out of your car to open up the trunk, all in the name of getting your toothbrush; and 2) you can avoid having to open up your trunk from the outside for simple items when pulling over in what could possibly be a "questionable area" late at night, just to relieve yourself of that gosh-awful feeling on your teeth. Collapsible rear seats leading to the trunk of your Road Warrior Vehicle from inside the passenger area of your car is as much a safety feature as it is a convenience.

What to Keep *Near You* While Driving

As for the rest of your traveling items, I highly recommend keeping the following Road Trip Essentials within close proximity of you at all times. (In the front passenger side seat of the car, if you're traveling alone, is a great location!):

Your Spiral Bound U.S. or North America Road Atlas – The spiral bound atlas seems the most efficient when driving because I find it easier to flip through with one hand, when necessary, but that's just my opinion. In addition, with a spiral bound atlas you rarely have to worry about breaking the binding loose from the rest of the pages if you're flipping through it in a hurry.

A Cooler for Sodas, Water, Sandwiches, Munchies, and Candy Bars! – I like to place this item in the floorboard of the passenger's side seat with the opening end facing the passenger side seat for easy access while driving down the road. I find this makes it easier to drive long stretches without having to pull over, if you don't want or need to, just to grab something to drink.

CD's, MP3 Players, and DVD's - (Though, you shouldn't be watching TV while you're driving anyway!) – Usually I find that keeping a travel flipping book for my CD's in the passenger side seat is the best course of action, because let's face it, if the music is getting old, it has got to change and it has got to change now! Not 30 miles from now (especially late at night)...and since you now know how to change a CD, or change the songs on your MP3 Player, without having to take your eyes off the road (*since you practiced "knowing your car like you know your own body" in the driveway before you left for your road trip*) there's nothing wrong with changing those tunes NOW!

Cell Phone, Cell Phone Car Charger, and Cell Phone Headset – These portable communication items are critical to the Road Warrior Princess' survival. I recommend keeping your cell phone car charger plugged into the power source plug (car cigarette lighter) at all times, so that in the event you're talking on the cell phone and the battery becomes low, you won't have to take your eyes off the road to figure out where the power source plug is located.

Second – More and more states are requiring a cell phone headset be used if you are talking on the phone while operating your car, and regardless of whether or not this new law has taken effect in your home state, I strongly recommend using this cell phone feature if you plan on talking while driving. The more control you have over your vehicle's steering controls while traveling along the Great Open Road, the safer you are because you never know when you'll come across a traffic jam (yes, even when out on the Open Road you run into these…you just don't want to *literally* run into them)! So CELL PHONE HEADSETS! Use them! They're great to have – especially if that friend that just loves to talk for hours calls you while you're on the Open Road…then you won't have to be rude by hanging up on her just because you need both of your hands to round those corners on a winding stretch of road going up or down a beautiful mountainside; unless of course, she's not *that good* of a friend and you really do want to have an excuse to get her off the phone anyway! I'm just joking! However, all jokes aside, the handsfree cell phone devices available on the open market are as much about ensuring your safety as they are about convenience.

Bottom line – When it comes to Open Road Communications - Make sure you're prepared for *any* driving situation by keeping these cell phone items charged, hooked up, and readily available *near you* when traveling!

A Digital or Film Camera - Keep a camera readily available in the passenger's side seat or on the floorboard of the car because the Open Road has some of *the most amazingly beautiful* sights I can possibly think of that this country has to offer with photo opportunities galore! So, BRING YOUR CAMERA along for the journey! You never know when you might need it!

Sunscreen – California's Sun is HOT! Simply driving up I-5 from Los Angeles can scorch your left arm within an hour or two if you don't put sunscreen on the arm hanging out the window facing the sun. I learned this lesson the hard way, so I pass this "School of Hard Knocks" lesson onto you – Keep sunscreen in your car at all times! If you have storage in a center console armrest, that's a great place to keep a small tube of sunscreen so you have easy access to it while you're driving. Inside your glove box is another great location!

Road Warrior Tip: Now that we know what should *be near the driver's seat* in your Road Warrior Vehicle, this leads us to one VERY IMPORTANT RULE! When traveling alone, if you're sleeping (whether in your car or at a motel/hotel) or when you are away from your car, keep your valuables, such as your Purse, CD's, DVD's, MP3 Player, Cell Phone, and Camera out of sight of those that will be walking near your car. This is especially important when you're sleeping in your car. If your guard is down, make sure your valuables are out of sight so that nobody decides to break your car window to take *just whatever happens to be sitting within arm's reach of the window inside your car.*

On a final note, just remember that keeping everything you need while on the road either well organized or within close proximity of your person is half the battle. If you have to take your eyes off the road to do something (Example: FINDING *and* putting on lipstick), as a safety precaution, always wait until you've stopped the car to perform these tasks.

What to Keep *On You* "Just In Case"

This is a topic I wasn't really sure where to put it, but it is such a valuable lesson that I think it needs to be said, and can be said here just as well as anywhere else in the book. I'd like to talk with you about the importance of keeping your Driver's License and spare money or an emergency credit card on you at all times when traveling. For guys, this is pretty simple, they always keep their wallet in their back or front pants pockets, unfortunately, women's clothing doesn't always accommodate for this sort of convenience. Though, however you decide to keep your Driver's License (I.D.) and Emergency Money on you, whether it's in a wrist wallet, in a pants pocket, or wherever you find most comfortable, it is very important that you always keep these two items on you at all times when you are traveling!

There are so many things that can happen to you when you are out on the Open Road, that it is just good common sense advice. If you've ever been unfortunate enough to be involved in a serious auto accident or ever had your car stolen when all you wanted to do was just run into a restroom real quick (without your purse), then you know what I mean. Specifically in a car accident situation, depending on how bad it is, you may not even be conscious enough to grab your purse, or your purse may have been destroyed in the jumbled mess of shredded car parts that "use to be" your Road Warrior Vehicle, during the accident.

For just these very reasons, I always keep my I.D. and some form of Emergency Funds on me because *I have been* one of those unfortunate souls, and had I needed to tell people where my wallet or purse was located in the wreckage, well, let's just say I wasn't in any state of mind to do that at the time. So for your own safety, keep your

I.D. *and* your Emergency Funds on you at all times when exploring the Adventures of the Open Road! It is a key to your survival if things turn out "not as planned".

Simple Rule 3

Don't Ever

Let Other People

Intimidate You!

Rule #3 – Don't Ever Let Other People Intimidate You!

Most important, never allow anybody *not* traveling with you to talk you out of knowing where you are going – even if you're not entirely sure where that is just yet yourself! You are always in control!

There is a common misconception that just because you are a woman, you shouldn't be allowed to travel long distances by yourself. NOT TRUE!

Road Warrior Story - I started out this book by telling you that I took my first Die-hard Road Warrior Adventure at the age of 18. Specifically, it was no sooner than I turned 18, I was already in the car and ready to go explore the world! My family and friends, even my boss said, "Uh, I don't know that this is such a good idea, Deb. You're a little blonde driving down to California in a little red car all by yourself – you could get hurt, or approached by the wrong people." This was true. I could have been approached by the "wrong kind of people", and believe me, I have had my share of weird experiences along my journeys, but I also get those same weird experiences just walking outside my door here in New Jersey. The point is, you're going to encounter whatever strange people you're going to encounter in this life regardless of whether or not you go on a road trip, so you may as well get out there and go explore the world if that's what your heart desires. Just don't let anybody tell you different!

Simple Rule 4

Tips, Tricks,

And Very Solid Advice

About Spending The Night Alone

During Your Road Warrior

Adventures!

Rule #4 – Tips, Tricks, and Very Solid Advice About Spending the Night Alone During Your Road Warrior Adventures

I'd like to take this opportunity to say something I rarely ever say - My friends, family members, and yes, even my old boss *had good reason to advise me not to go on a road trip by myself.* There are some crazy people out there. There are people who will see a woman traveling alone and think you're somebody they'd like to try to pester (to put it kindly). The Golden Rule for this situation is that a Road Warrior Princess is ALWAYS aware of her surroundings and she *knows* how to take care of herself – The Road Warrior Princess IS Always Prepared for ANY Situation!

This is Your Road Trip! Your Adventure! Your Journey! Your Time! Your Life! And don't let *anybody* get in the way of you doing and experiencing what you want!

With that said, there are a handful of safety tips and general rules that I live by and will NOT break when I'm traveling alone. By implementing these Simple Rules into your traveling arrangements, you may feel more confident that *you can* find safe passage too.

The Truth About Rest Areas

The fact is Rest Areas are great! On the flipside, how many stories have we heard or read about in the newspaper that read along the lines of "Woman Disappears From Rest Area"? The truth is, if you plan to REST with your eyes closed in a REST AREA, as a woman traveling alone, you need to follow a few Simple Guidelines to ensure your own safety:

Guideline #1 About Rest Areas - Don't ever stop in a rest area that has no other cars parked in the parking lot! This should go without saying, but with tens of thousands of miles of cross-country driving experience under my belt, I can tell you right now, stopping at a rest area where you're the only person there is NEVER a good idea because you never know who may pull up next to you.

Road Warrior Story - This portion of Road Warrior Princess Rule #4 came about because one time *I did* pull into a rest area where I was the only person there, thinking of course that everything would be just fine, and just as I thought all would be well, a van pulled up next to me and six convicts in chains stepped out of the van and headed up the walkway toward the facilities. Now maybe I've watched too many jailbreak movies, but it was a very uncomfortable feeling at the time and I have created this rule and lived by it when traveling alone ever since.

Road Warrior Tip: While we're talking about this subject, I'd like to address the possibilities of large trucks and truck drivers. First off, I think truck drivers are some of your best friends on the Open Road. They know the road and they're always around. For the most part, they're all pretty good people, but nuzzling your car in with a bunch of semi-trucks so you can rest isn't always the best idea (unless you're driving a big truck pulling a trailer or are driving a moving truck). The truth is, the drivers of these larger trucks can't always see your smaller vehicle down there when they're just as tired as you are from traveling long distances. So to avoid dangerous situations, keep your car in the "Cars Only" section of the rest area, and if there aren't any other CARS parked overnight in the "Cars Only" section of the rest area, keep moving until you find the next rest area that does have at least 2-3 other cars parking nearby. It is in your own best interest and for your safety as a Road Warrior Princess to never park alone!

Guideline #2 About Rest Areas - When traveling alone, now that we know to check and make sure at least 2-3 other cars are parked in the rest area (preferably other people that are also resting during their travels) - the big question: Where to park your car for optimal safety while getting some shuteye when out on the Open Road alone?

    The answer to this simple question is *smack dab in front of the garbage cans near the main entrance walkway to the rest area's facilities.* This location is typically right in the center of the parking lot next to the sidewalk and will typically have a lot of foot traffic.

I know it seems like this would be the loudest and most obnoxious place to rest with all sorts of people constantly going to the garbage cans to throw out the garbage from their cars – However, by strategically placing yourself (and your vehicle) in the highest traffic area of the rest area you are reducing your chances of being disturbed by an *unwanted intruder* while you rest. Sure, a few people will look at you while you sleep, but people with ill-willed intentions are less likely to bother you while you sleep if you're parked right under a light and right in front of a garbage can where other people will notice if something suspicious is happening to you and/or your vehicle too!

Now, this guideline is not *just* about parking in front of the garbage cans or near the main walkway, *the true emphasis here* is to make sure you are in the center of things. That your car is strategically placed in the highest traffic areas, not off to the far sides of the parking lot where things are a little quieter. The reason we don't want to be where there is less traffic and things are quieter, is because that is exactly where someone with bad intentions would like you to be when you're asleep and your defenses are down.

I'm sure you're thinking by now, I just mentioned that right in front of the garbage cans is typically right under the lights. Yes, when you park smack dab in front of the garbage cans that are near the main walkway to the facilities, you will also be smack dab under the lights! Although this location is not exactly an *ideal situation* for getting a good night's sleep, this next piece of advice about rest areas helps resolve this inconvenience while protecting you from harm's way.

Guideline #3 About Rest Areas - Find a hat you love and bring it with you every time you travel on the road. This is a great way to not only control those bad hair days, but it also serves as a deterrent while you are sleeping. Think like an ill-willed person for a second. Anybody who will want to bother you while you are sleeping is probably in need of finding some sense of false power for his or her life. Since it is easier for a perpetrator to feel power over someone when they can look their victim in the face; we will take away the initial intrigue, by covering our eyes with the bill of a hat - and Voila! Now these potentially ill-willed perpetrators can just keep on moving because they have no clue, who or what kind of a powerful woman they're about ready to cross paths with, should they disturb your sleep!

As a Road Warrior Princess, you are a powerful, decisive woman of your own free will to choose who gets the privilege of being near you, and who is denied such graces. Keep the ill-willed wanderers from getting curious and act like the cowboys of The Old West; drop that hat down over your eyes and get a good night's rest!

Guideline #4 About Rest Areas - Power side view mirrors are your security system when you sleep. Earlier in this book, I mentioned that power side view mirrors, which can be adjusted from inside the driver's side of the car, are a non-negotiable safety feature when finding the perfect Road Warrior Vehicle - and when you're traveling alone, power side view mirrors are *one of your best resources* for security.

Allow me to explain:

Before settling in for a good night's rest, lay your seat all the way back (in the position you will be laying down to sleep), then adjust your side view mirrors so that they are pointing in a more downward direction. Making these adjustments to your side view mirrors while lying down will allow you to see what is happening on the right and left sides of your vehicle while you are in the lying down position. Adjust your rear view mirror in the center of the car so you can see out the rear window while in the lying down position.

Once your mirrors are in place, should you hear a bump in the night, all you have to do is open your eyes, glance at all three of your mirrors to check for suspicious activity, if you see nothing, chances are, you're all right. This is a little trick I decided to incorporate into my traveling rules because with so many strange noises going on around me, I use to jump up panic-stricken at least a half a dozen times to see what was going on around me every time I'd pull over to get some rest. Then I started adjusting my mirrors, and now, if I hear something strange that sounds like it's happening right outside my car, I just glance at my mirrors; once I see that everything is okay, I can feel comfortable shutting my eyes again and am better able to relax so I can go back to sleep. It's a lot easier to stay in "sleepy mode" when I don't have to sit straight up, because then I want to throw my seat back up into the upright position, and if I do that, then my pillow gets messed up, my blanket gets in the way, and it's really just a screwy situation all of the way around! So, save yourself the aggravation, adjust your mirrors so you can take a quick glance around the car from the lying down position and you'll thank me for this advice later!

Guideline #5 About Rest Areas - So this begs the question: What do you do with those ignition keys while you sleep? Do you leave them in the ignition while you sleep, or do you take them out of the ignition?

The Simple Rule of the Road Warrior Princess is to never allow anybody to think they have a chance to steal your car away from you (even when you're sleeping).

If you leave your keys dangling from the ignition while you sleep, all an ill-willed person has to do to get your car is get rid of you because your keys are dangling right there in the vehicle's ignition turn switch. Now if you're sleeping with the keys out of sight, but easily accessible should you need to leave in a hurry, then someone looking through the window cannot see your keys and things no longer appear as easy to get your car away from you. At the same time, you will still have quick and easy access to them, should you need to use them in a hurry.

As far as clothing that works well to create this sort of convenient, yet safer, situation - The pullover sweatshirt with a pocket in the front (commonly referred to as a "Hoodie") works great for not only providing a pocket to store your keys in while sleeping; these sweatshirts are also super comfy and warm to wear while resting! I love these sweatshirts when I travel because even during the summer months, it can still get cold at night. If your keys are safely on your person, but within easy reach, should you need to leave in a hurry, then you are traveling as a Smart Road Warrior Princess should be – with Safety in Mind!

The Exception to Guideline #5

Now, what if it's the dead of winter and you need your heater to run while you're sleeping? This would be the exception to the rule, not the norm. If it is the dead of winter, and depending on the circumstances, as well as, the given environment of where you are parked, then yes, by all means, in the dead of winter, please, turn on your car and let that heater run! However, if the engine is off, take those keys out of the ignition!

With respect to resting in your car during cold outside temperatures or when traveling during the winter months, if you must do this (as oppose to staying elsewhere to rest, such as a motel), then my advice here is to first always thoroughly heat up your Road Warrior Vehicle (to almost too warm) before going to sleep. I find that (usually) if I just turn the heater on high, let it run while I'm getting settled in and then turn off the car while I sleep; it tends to stay "just right" inside the car for a few hours while I take a quick rest.

All in all, and with the exception of resting in your car during winter months or cold weather, turning off the car engine and keeping the keys out of the ignition while sleeping serves two purposes really: The first reason is safety; the second reason is fuel conservation. When you sleep with the engine running, you could very well wake up with a near empty tank of gas if you didn't just fill up before pulling over for the night. A car that idles for an extended period of time uses up a lot of fuel!

Guideline #6 About Rest Areas - As women, we possess a unique gift called *Intuition*, and when it comes to getting some shuteye in a rest area, your intuition IS your very best indication as to whether or not a particular rest area is a good area for you to rest your eyes for the night. Follow your gut instincts about rest areas. If it has a good vibe, rest your eyes and wake up refreshed in the morning, and if you're getting a bad vibe from an area, move on. Trust your intuition! There is nothing wrong with pulling into a rest area, and then deciding it's just not right for you to remain there.

Road Warrior Stories - I can't even tell you how many times I've had this happen to me, particularly in the state of Wyoming. For whatever reason, I can never seem to get a good feeling about rest areas along I-90 in this state. However, on my 10th trip across the country, I finally found a great rest area that has a good vibe to it and now that I know where it is, I've marked it on my map and will always try to make it there first.

Another time was more severe because I thought I'd never find a place to rest. This time happened while I was driving through a massive blizzard. To give you the entire picture of what happened, it all started because I was driving from New York to Idaho, which is about a 2 ½-day trip when driven straight through, both day and night, throughout the length of the journey.

There is a rest area about 70 miles east of Chicago where I usually pull in for rest when driving cross-country, and all was going well, that is until I pulled into this rest area. Just as I was settling in for the night, I received a call from my parents. Frantic because they had been watching the news, my parents relayed the information they'd heard on their weather report and insisted that I needed to "get going" and head north because there was a massive storm on its way to Chicago.

First of all, I was tired! I didn't want to start driving again! I had already been driving for over 13 hours. It was *sleepy time*! But! They insisted, as my father encouraged me to "move on" by explaining, "Well, you can either keep moving tonight and get through Chicago before the storm hits, or you can stay in Chicago for 2-3 days because once the storm hits, you won't be able to get through." In hindsight, my father was dead-on accurate with his advice, because after the storm hit, it did take the City of Chicago 2-3 days to clear all the roads and get traffic moving again. So in spite of my weary driving state, I pushed on – this is how I wound up in the situation of trying to find a good rest area and not having a good vibe, then moving on, and so forth.

The storm was bad and just as I was hitting the Northwest Perimeter of Chicago's City Limits the snowflakes began to fall. Apparently, the Officials for the City of Chicago also knew this would be a bad storm because they had 20 to 30 snowplows and salting trucks safeguarding the Western City Limits of Chicago from Mother Nature's wrath like a battalion readying for war – and it was with a mighty fierce wrath that Mother Nature struck that night too. I'll never forget the feelings I felt while driving out of the Chicago City Limits that night. I was terrified as I stared at the blinding snowfall in front of me while saying "good-bye" to the guardian snowplows behind me with their bright flashing yellow lights still flickering in the rear view mirror. Although I wished to stay, nonetheless, I drove away into the disorienting pitch-black night.

I'd never stopped in a rest area in Wisconsin before, but I knew I had at least another 2-3 hours drive before I arrived at Madison, Wisconsin, and it was a rough 2-3 hours at that. As I drove down the freeway, the lines defining the lanes on the freeway became less evident, and within an hour, trying to figure out where the freeway was actually leading me became even less obvious.

Eventually, I found myself in a situation where it was just me and what I was praying was still the road. At the time, it felt like all I could figure out was that there were trees to the right and to the left of me, and whatever was the flat snowy white patch forming a smoother path in the center (through deductive reasoning of course) must have been the freeway. Then the craziness began – the truck drivers and their huge 18-wheel tractor-trailer trucks started passing me in droves! Here I was, a little passenger car plowing 2 feet of snow with my front bumper, and all I could do was just drive as close to the tree lined perimeter on the right side of the flakey flat surface as I felt comfortable doing while heavily praying for my own safety as each 18-wheeler spit up a whirlwind of blinding snow flake flurries around my car with each and every pass on the freeway.

I was desperate for a rest area by 2 a.m. I'd been driving for nearly 16 hours straight through and my eyes were glazed over from having been blinded by Mother Nature and a league of inconsiderate truck drivers (or so I felt that night) – It was definitely time to pull over!

The big problem: How did I know if "that" particular white snowy path leading off the "assumed" freeway was really an off-ramp and not just a ditch off the side of the road? Everything was plastered in white and visible road signs were a thing of the past at this point. The fact was, I didn't know if what I had seen was really an off-ramp or the ditch lining the side of the road, and so the journey continued.

Driving down the road, it seemed like every road sign potentially telling me how much further I had to go until the next town was caked in white blankets of snow. I had no clue how far I'd driven, nor how much further I had to drive until I would eventually find shelter from the storm. By 3:30 a.m., the trees had guarded the storm enough that I was *finally* able to recognize what looked like a rest area to the right. Plus! - I was driving slow enough (after all, I was plowing 2-3 feet of snow with my front bumper at that point) that I didn't need much notice to hang a quick right off the road and into the rest area.

This rest area was beautiful under the snow fallen night. The rest area parking lot was covered in nearly 2 ½ feet of untouched snow. It was lying like a blanket and glistened with a sparkling warm welcome under the tungsten orange glow of streetlights in the cold dark night. Not a single tire track in sight, except for mine now, of course. Nobody had been here. I was the only one. The snow covered trees illuminated under the rest area park lights as the snow fell around the car. I was so tired that my eyes burned from staring at the blinding road for so long. At this point, I just almost didn't care if I broke my own rule, but I had that "funny" (peculiar) feeling. You know, that unsettling feeling you get in your heart and in the pit of your stomach when you *just know* something isn't quite right? Well, I had it. So I stayed up and wrote in my journal for a while. I figured if something "screwy" or strange were about to happen (like the blizzard I'd been trapped in for the past 4 ½ hours hadn't been screwy enough), then it would happen before I decided to fall asleep for the night.

Sure as I was writing in my journal, wouldn't you know it? A white van pulled up! Now I don't have anything against white vans in general, but all things considered, if I'm the only person in a rest area and a white van decides to pull up right next to me and then the driver sits there and stares at me for a while, well, that's a clue for me to move on. Hence, I put away my journal, rubbed my eyes, and headed back out to the Open Road. The way I figured it, whatever was out on the Open Road that night had to be better than sleeping somewhere I did not feel safe.

About an hour later, the trees blocked Mother Nature's fury one more time for me. This time it was just enough to uncover a road sign that said "Lodging Next Right". At least this time I knew that whatever white blanket leading off the freeway I saw next would most likely be an off-ramp. A few minutes later, I found myself "skiing" into a small quiet town on all four tires. All but a couple of the streetlights were dark in this small town, and the "lodging" didn't even have a light on either at this wee hour of the morning. Knowing that I couldn't very well keep going much longer without getting some shuteye, I decided that pulling into the parking lot of this "lodging" facility might be my best chance to get some sleep. So that's what I did. I pulled in, got all comfy, adjusted my mirrors, and settled in for "a long winter's nap" (or at least I was hoping for a "few hours" anyway)!

Just as I was getting comfortable and began dozing off to sleep, I had this really petrifying and quick dream of somebody breaking into my car while I was asleep. Hmmm…intuition or hallucination? After all, I had been driving for almost 19 hours solid at this point. Nonetheless, I didn't stay to question what I was feeling, so I sat back up, put on my seat belt, opened a new can of highly caffeinated soda, and headed back out to the Open Road. Besides, the sun would come up in an hour or two, and by then I'd be able to see better, right? Not so, but once the sun came up early that following morning, I did finally find a rest area with many other parked cars camping out during the storm and I was finally able to get a good 5 hours of sleep.

The moral of the story is, follow your "gut instinct", and listen to your intuition (even if you are severely tired). Chances are, if you've got a feeling that you're not in a safe area, or that there is something *just not quite right* about a particular rest area or lodging area, chances are, your intuition can see something that your physical eyes cannot. A Great Road Warrior Princess knows to listen to *and* to follow all of her senses, not just the basic five. As women, we are in touch with this wonderful sense, so use it!

Guideline #7 About Rest Areas - East of the Mississippi vs. West of the Mississippi

As a first general rule: West of the Mississippi typically feels safer to me than rest areas that are located East of the Mississippi. This is not to say that you can't get some good shuteye if you are traveling on the East Coast, it just means do as a Great Road Warrior Princess should always do - Always Know Your Surroundings Before Going to Sleep Anywhere!

As a second general rule: I NEVER stop in the state of Virginia to shut my eyes. I'm not sure why, I just get the worst vibe at every rest area I've ever been to in this particular state. Some states are weird like that, plus in Virginia, they even know that their rest areas aren't very safe, because they post signs everywhere stating that overnight parking is not allowed. So if you're ever traveling through Virginia, just heed these signs as good advice to move on, and now that you know, you can adjust your Road Warrior Adventure Plans accordingly!

Guideline #8 About Rest Areas - Hitchhikers and weird people (according to one's own personal definitions) that like to "hangout" at rest areas.

Yes, most of us believe that hitchhikers no longer exist. After all, it's been a long time since the 1970s but on any given Road Warrior Travel Day you can find at least a half a dozen hitchhikers walking idly by the freeway in the big sky country of Montana or along the scenic wilderness side roads, freeways, and highways of Oregon. As a Road Warrior Princess, even if he or she looks cute, do not pick that person up! It's a good rule to live by – after all, your Road Warrior Adventure should run by *your* agenda, NOT by somebody else's, and when you pick up a hitchhiker, now your adventure just became somebody else's adventure, not yours.

As for weird people that like to "hangout" at rest areas, the fact is, this is true. With the world becoming as populated as it has become, most rest areas are located only within a handful of miles of a nearby town or city (except for remote places like South Dakota, etc.). In general, though, you will find that rest areas are located within a half hour or so of a nearby town - Mainly, because the people maintaining the rest areas typically do live nearby the rest area they maintain. With this said, be cautious of people that look like they are not traveling as you are traveling.

Road Warrior Story - I'll never forget the time I woke up in a rest area in Oregon, only to find someone knocking on my window. As I looked up, there was an old guy with long gray hair and a long gray beard sitting on a bicycle staring back at me through my driver's side window. After rubbing the sleepy out of my eyes, I yelled through the window (remember, don't ever roll your window down for a stranger, because it is considered an "invite"), "what do you want?" He wanted to know if I had something on me, and I was like, "Dude, somebody needs to tell this guy the '60s are over!" Ironically, him asking me for something I didn't have wasn't the weird part of this story; it was the fact that an old guy was riding a bicycle around a rest area that I was under the impression to be located *many* miles away from any towns that wigged me out the most. Hence, know your surroundings and stay cautious around those that look like they might not be traveling long distances, as you are, especially when getting some shuteye at a rest area.

The Truth About "Mini-Hotels"

The fact is, sometimes whether you usually enjoy a good night's sleep in a motel or hotel, or you're going for the Die-hard Road Warrior Experience on a small budget, sometimes you just can't find that "perfect place" to settle down for a good night's rest. In this case, it's good to know your options when it comes to the "Mini-Hotel" (as I like to call them).

What is a "Mini-Hotel"?

Basically, the "Mini-Hotel" is your typical big name hotel chain, only "expressed" or converted into some sort of a *downsized* version of their regular inn or travel lodging experience normally offered to customers.

However, every so often you may find yourself in a part of the country where all you can find are "mom and pop" type lodging facilities because Corporate America has yet to move in and take over that particular area of the country, just yet. Regardless of the type of facility you choose to rest and relax in, a few words of advice:

Road Warrior Tip: The big name "expresses" along the highways and freeways of the nation will always charge you more than you really want to pay, and the tragedy is that you will pay their ridiculous prices because your eyes are so tired and bloodshot from staring at hundreds of miles of road that you really don't want to drive around forever looking for the best deal to save a few bucks.

The Best Way to Deal with THIS Situation...

Travel Coupons - Carry a few travel coupons with you for the various states you think you will be traveling through – and if you didn't plan this before you left for your Road Warrior Adventure – NO PROBLEM – Remember those wonderful rest areas? Most of the time, they have a State Travel Coupon Book or Magazine sitting in a news (type) stand somewhere near the restrooms. Whenever you stop at a rest area, just look for the coupon book, and grab one for "just in case". For those of you that have a roadside assistance program membership, you can always find great deals with your local office if you let them know just before you leave for your adventure that you're looking for coupons.

Location! Location! Location! - The further the "Mini-Hotel" is located away from the freeway, the better the rate! (It's also a little more quiet!)

Single Owner-Operated Motels - As for those "mom and pop" type motels: Did you ever watch a scary movie that takes place at a small single owner "motel" with a flickering sign? Perhaps I've seen too many movies, or just had too many unpleasant real life experiences, but these small "mom and pop" or single owner-operated type motels are what I call "The *Scary* Motels". Typically, they don't cost much less than a "Mini-Hotel", and in this day and age, unless the place looks exceptionally well cared for (and many of them are), don't bother stopping at one for a good night's sleep if you are a woman traveling alone. There are much safer options out there. Now, I don't mean to offend any reader that might own or operate a motel of this size or type, this is just my opinion. I have bought into this type of lodging several times out of desperation for a good night's sleep, and it has *never* resulted in a good night's sleep. I usually wind up leaving only a few hours after check-in to go find a nice rest area down the road with less money in my pocket than when I pulled into the motel, not to mention far crankier because now it's that much later and I'm *still* looking for a good place to rest for the night.

The Continental Divide - (That's not the one I'm talking about!) – In my experience and for whatever reason, if the lodging facility offers a REALLY GOOD free continental breakfast, then the service is always *that much better (and so is the rest)*. Although I have traveled to many places, the very best and most well cared for continental breakfast I ever had was at a "Mini-Hotel" in Gillette, Wyoming. That was a Great Continental Breakfast! (Not to mention, I had a great night's sleep too!)

The Truth About Gas Stations at Night

Yes, I'll admit it, I have pulled into a gas station before and rested there for the night. There are only a few times I've done this in my life, and those times were during severe winter weather conditions up in the Big Horn Mountains of Wyoming. If you should find yourself in this situation; finding a gas station to be a necessary sleeping arrangement while on your own Road Warrior Princess Adventure, I *strongly recommend* you park your Road Warrior Vehicle somewhere near, yet out of the way of, truckers (and make sure there are at least 3 or more trucks resting for the night at that same gas station).

In addition, I wouldn't recommend utilizing this sort of sleeping arrangement unless you plan on waking up around 5 a.m. and want to get back on the road *really early*. Beware! First thing in the morning, those trucks can be VERY LOUD! As always, unless this is a last resort, I wouldn't recommend sleeping at a gas station as being a good idea for a Road Warrior Princess.

This leads us to our next vital Road Warrior Princess Rule...

Simple Rule 5

The Truth About Where The Safest

Gas Stations Are Located!

Rule #5 – The Truth About Where the Safest Gas Stations are Located

Yes, there are some stretches of America that are paved in corporate or government fees in order for us to travel the Great Open Road these days, and one of the biggest benefits of the Toll Road System is that they provide service areas for you every so many miles where you can eat, stretch, shop, and get gas - All in one happy little travel plaza! Personally, I don't like paying tolls to travel the Open Road, but the "one stop shopping" travel plazas *are* the upside, if there has to be one.

The downside is that if you have never traveled for long distances down a non-toll road, it begs the question: How do you know which part of a town is safe enough so you can pull off the highway and get gas?

The answer to this question is a simple, yet silly sounding, rule that has ALWAYS kept me safe. Whether I needed to refuel in broad daylight or in the middle of the night, I've never had a problem so long as I've followed this one Simple Rule:

If there is a Major Brand Name Petroleum (Gas) Station and a Major Franchised Food Chain on the same exit, take that exit to get gas.

So what if you don't like the particular food chain that is listed on the exit sign? It's a good question, but the point isn't about getting food at the same time you get your gas, so much as it is about the gas station's location, ease of getting on and off of the freeway (without getting lost), and the location's safety environment at night, especially late at night. As a Road Warrior Princess Traveling the Mighty Open Road Alone, your safety is priority number one!

Simply put, in my experience, and for whatever reason, gas stations that are located next to these fast food giants of the franchising world appear to always be located in a safer area of town than gas stations located next to other food supplies, or no food supply for that matter. Like I said, it sounds silly, but after 10 plus years of Die-hard Road Warrior Adventures, this rule has always kept me safe, and to me, that means this Simple Rule is important enough to put in this book. Besides, it's not like there is a shortage of *major* conglomerate brand name fast food chains around the country. I've been just about everywhere in this country and traveled across, over, up, and down many different side roads, highways, and freeways around this nation. Because of these experiences, I can honestly say, I have never, not a once, been unable to *find a Major Franchised Food Chain located next to a Major Brand Name Petroleum (Gas) Station within a block or two of each other* whenever I've needed to refuel in an unfamiliar location, and this Simple Rule has always kept me safe.

How To Get

More Bang For Your Buck

At The Pump!

Rule #6 – How to Get More Bang for Your Buck at the Pump!

As of the writing of this book, gas prices in the United States have been fluctuating between slightly below $2.00 a gallon and a soaring unheard of $4.00 PLUS a gallon with no consistency or reassurance for when a relatively steady price range for gasoline can be expected to stabilize in the future. With such uncertainty in fuel prices and no end in sight for our economic woes – These volatile prices and harsh economic conditions are creating a financial drain on the American household wallet. So this begs the question: How do you go on a Road Warrior Adventure and let your hair flow wild while embracing the Open Road when your budget is already too tight? The answer to this fear is simple…Get more bang for your buck by extending your fuel mileage in between each and every fuel up at the pump!

The trick to winning the never-ending battle between your wallet and how much fuel your Road Warrior Vehicle's engine *wants* to consume is really nothing more than maintaining a delicate balance between *properly maintaining your car* and becoming more conscientious about *the way you drive*!

Properly Maintaining Your Car is Half the Battle

Tire Pressure – If you do nothing else that is recommended in this chapter – this one tidbit of advice alone can automatically improve the number of miles per gallon you get out of your car…each and every tank!

As a Great Road Warrior Princess already knows from reading the chapters earlier in this book – checking and maintaining proper air pressure in your tires is ESSENTIAL to Road Warrior Princess Safety. However, the added benefit of checking your tire inflation regularly to ensure that your tire pressures are, at the very least, set to the minimum manufacturer's specifications is that you can dramatically improve your miles per gallon (MPG) as you drive around.

The philosophy behind this tip is relatively simple - The more resistance your tires have to endure while rolling down the road; the harder your engine has to work to keep those tires rolling. Thus, the more gas (or alternative energy source) your Road Warrior Vehicle's engine has to use in order to work hard enough to keep you going down the road safely! So when checking your tires, just remember that the higher the air pressure in your tires (not to exceed the MAX psi embossed on the sidewalls of your tires); the less rolling resistance your car will endure while driving. The less rolling resistance your tires have to endure; the less your engine has to work to maintain speed; and…*the less your engine has to work to maintain speed; the less fuel consumption used for Road Warrior Adventures!*

Clean Air Filters – By regularly checking the air filter under the hood on your car's engine and keeping it clean, you will improve the airflow in your engine and dramatically reduce the amount of resistance, and thus the amount of work, your engine has to do just to function properly.

Oil Changes – Not only does changing the oil regularly improve the power performance of your engine and reduce the likelihood of your car breaking down on you, but the value of regularly dumping out the old grimy gritty oil in your engine and replacing it with new clean smooth oil is that your engine operates with less resistance during regular operation. Thus, you use less fuel to accomplish the same performance when driving.

Road Warrior Tip: More recently, there are a variety of "Lifetime" Oil Filters out on the market now that claim to improve gas (or fuel) mileage. I'm mentioning it in this book because my brother-in-law is using them on his vehicles during the writing of this book and since he is really satisfied with his decision to use them, this seems like a tip worth addressing. Therefore, if you feel like changing your oil yourself *and* cleaning out the same oil filter each and every time you change your oil, there are many claims on the market that these "Lifetime" Oil Filters may also help improve your fuel MPG.

Engine Belts – Checking and ensuring proper maintenance of the various engine belts is one simple method to dramatically reducing the amount of energy consumption your Road Warrior Vehicle's engine utilizes to keep you cruising comfortably down the road at the optimal speeds to which you have become accustomed!

The philosophy behind this is simple - If the belts on your engine are old, loose, worn-out or are repeatedly "slipping" by even just a fraction of an inch while under heavy strain and high RPM (revolutions per minute), then your engine will have to work EXTRA HARD to compensate for the slippage happening with those loose, worn-out, and "slacking" engine belts in order to provide you with the same performance. In combination with these other tips, keep those engine belts new (ish), tight, and inspected regularly for optimal performance and you may find that your fuel usage has dramatically reduced while embracing the Open Road!

Spark Plugs or Wires – When keeping your car maintained, changing your spark plugs or wires at the regular recommended intervals for your Road Warrior Vehicle can also prevent your car from using more fuel than it should. Oftentimes, misfiring cylinders caused by faulty spark plugs or wires can reduce your engine's efficiency, and thus, reduce your efforts to boost your MPG. So keep those cylinders firing correctly and you'll be well on your way to getting more bang for your buck between fill ups at the fuel pump!

The *Way You Drive* is the Other Half of the Battle!

There are many theories out there about *how* you drive your car affecting your ability to receive either "good" or "poor" fuel mileage per gallon. Consequently, I could write another entire book on just this topic alone. However, for our purposes, the following are a handful of very useful Simple Rules for the Road Warrior Princess when it comes to "how" you drive so that you too may enjoy the benefits of reducing your Road Warrior Vehicle's energy usage and fuel consumption.

How You Drive Starts with *What You Drive* - *What you drive* can mean anything from whether you drive a heavy, boxy, gas-guzzling SUV vs. a more aerodynamic compact economy car. *What you drive* also refers to whether you drive a Hybrid Road Warrior Vehicle that relies on both batteries and gasoline to generate energy; or do you drive a diesel vehicle; or do you drive a strictly "traditional" gas-guzzling machine down the Open Road during your Road Warrior Adventures? Furthermore, *what you drive* can also refer to whether or not you drive a vehicle with an Automatic Transmission, a Manual Transmission (also called a "Stick Shift"), or does your Road Warrior Vehicle have a transmission that is a combination of the two, such as a Semi-Automatic Transmission?

So What's the Difference?
... and How Do These "Differences" Affect the Way You Drive?

SUV vs. Compact Econocar (Short for "Economy Car") – When embarking on the Open Road – the more room you have to store all of your favorite travel tools, clothes, souvenirs, and other various Road Warrior Adventure essentials, acquired both *for* and *during* your trip, makes the Sports Utility Vehicle (SUV) an ideal choice for storage space depending on *where* and *for how long* you plan on embracing The Great Unknown.

HOWEVER, during the writing of this book, considering the dire situation with the United States and Global Economies, when it comes to the enormous price tag at the gas pump to fill up these low MPG gas-guzzling beauties, utilizing your mammoth SUV for such Road Warrior Adventures can really put a crimp on your Road Warrior Adventure Budget!

Not only does the less-than-aerodynamic design of these larger vehicles increase the amount of wind resistance encountered while driving down the road, but the larger engine size and heavier weight of these vehicles are also factors that tend to require more fuel consumption. These are things to consider before choosing an SUV as your primary Road Warrior Vehicle because these design features have a direct influence on how much fuel consumption your adventures will require.

Alternatively, the smaller, more compact econocar design is an excellent lighter weight fuel-efficient Road Warrior Vehicle because of its more aerodynamic body design to help reduce "drag" (or wind resistance). Plus! – When driven a certain way, these smaller more economical travelers of the Mighty Open Road can sometimes even produce results that nearly double the manufacturer's quoted mileage per gallon estimates for some smaller vehicle models.

The reason I say this, is because over the years I have designated two *different* gasoline-powered sporty lil' economy cars as my Road Warrior Vehicles during my many Great Road Warrior Adventures, and I am tickled pink to tell you that – YES! I was able to achieve well over 50 miles per gallon during my Road Warrior Adventures while using *only* good ol' fashioned gasoline! Wow! This phenomenal reduction in fuel usage during my nearly one dozen cross-country road trips was accomplished by not only my choice of Road Warrior Vehicle and desired manufacturer's features for my car, but was also a result of the *way* I drove my car across the country – of which we will discuss in a second, but first...

Does the Way You Fuel Your Vehicle Really Make a Difference?

Fuel Economy and How to Choose? – In the Era of "Green" Automotive Decision Making Choices, as consumers, we are incredibly confused by all of this talk about achieving greater fuel economy for our Road Warrior Adventures based on whether or not our vehicles run on Gasoline; uses a Hybrid mix of both Gas *and* Batteries; if it's a Plug-in Hybrid; if it has a Diesel Engine and runs on Biodiesel, such as Vegetable Oil, or does it run on Ethanol-Diesel; or does the vehicle run on Ethanol-Gasoline (also commonly referred to as E85 because it is a mixture of 85% Ethanol and 15% Gasoline)? – Better yet, is your Road Warrior Vehicle a Hydrogen Fuel-cell Vehicle; is it fueled by Natural Gas (CNG is CH4); or does it operate on an entirely different alternative fuel source altogether, such as 100% Ethanol that is derived from Sugarcane (which has become popular in Brazil)??? With so many choices, how does a Road Warrior Princess choose the *right* Road Warrior Vehicle and fuel source for her long sought adventures?

Although I could write an entire book on how these different fuel sources claim to increase MPG, the bottom line for a Road Warrior Princess to concern herself with when making such decisions is: How available is your fuel source as you travel the Open Road? If you have a Plug-in Hybrid car, will there be a way for you to "plug in" your car at night to recharge the batteries during your travels? Alternatively, if your Road Warrior Vehicle runs on Hydrogen or E85, are there enough "alternative fuel stations" on the travel route *you want to take* so that you can refuel along the way while still enjoying your fantastic new and improved MPG?

To help point you in the right direction when making these decisions about *just how available* many of these new fuel resources are for Coast to Coast (or North to South) traveling - In addition to many other great resources out on the Internet, staying up-to-date by viewing the U.S. Department of Energy's website is a great resource for comparing the benefits of using such alternative fuel sources for your Road Warrior Adventure needs. This site can also help you figure out and locate just exactly *how many* alternative fuel stations are accessible near the various locations you wish to travel, should you choose not to use a traditional "gasoline only" engine during your various Open Road Adventures! Also, for those of you traveling outside the United States of America, be sure to check with local government authorities to figure out how you can find this information for your travel planning.

In such a new, unexplored, and ever-changing "Green" Automotive Environment, these resources will most certainly help you better chart your course for both home and long distance Road Warrior Travel while empowering you to dramatically reduce your spending so that you too can truly embrace and enjoy the Open Road, just as a Daring Road Warrior Princess should be able to do - without suffering a large financial burden at the fuel pump!

How Does My Transmission Affect the Way I Drive?

Manual vs. Automatic vs. Semi-Automatic Transmissions – Some Road Warriors love to feel 100% in control at all times, and when it comes to *how* you drive your car for greater fuel-efficiency, the manual transmission is by far one of the *very best* ways to ensure you always have complete and total control over exactly how much or how little fuel you are using, at all times. Although the constant *pushing in* and *letting out* of the clutch can feel like a workout at the gym under various traffic conditions, the reason why a manual transmission gives you so much control is because you can opt to not engage the engine at various declines during your driving experience (which allows you to use less gas). You also have optimal control over how many RPM (revolutions per minute) your engine is engaging while traveling (where using fewer RPM typically helps conserve energy, and thus fuel). As well, you can have 100% control over maintaining and reducing speed without hitting the brakes all the time, which constant braking is one of the primary reasons most vehicles use so much fuel over the course of a long journey or during local stop-and-go traffic. With that said, I would like to point out that, in my experience, opting for driving a Road Warrior Vehicle with a manual transmission is just one of the many reasons I have been fortunate enough to achieve such great gas mileage over the years.

Alternatively, for those of you that frequently drive in heavy traffic conditions or extremely hilly driving environments (where it takes a certain amount of brilliantly timed coordination and sometimes "luck" to drive a stick shift up these roads), having an automatic transmission offers you the luxury of letting the car optimize your engine's RPM for you. However, you lose a lot of control over those prime "gas saver" moments along the travel terrain because the car is now entrusted to know how to optimize fuel consumption better than you (hence, you are giving up control).

Although having an automatic transmission was once considered a gas-guzzling choice (and the evidence was in the Environmental Protection Agency's (EPA) MPG ratings on fuel-efficiency for same make and model vehicles that had an automatic transmission vs. a manual transmission) - The good news is that in today's "Green" frenzy to find better ways of improving fuel-efficiency many of the newer vehicle's powertrain systems utilize what is called a continuously variable transmission (CVT). This advanced powertrain technology in newer vehicles allows the car to more closely match the transmission ratios with the optimum RPM range of the engine for better fuel-efficiency.

Without our having to *fully understand* just exactly *how* CVT works, this new technology means that even a vehicle with an automatic transmission has the potential ability to become far more fuel-efficient than previously believed. Thankfully, with these new strides in automotive technologies, this also means that auto manufacturers are finally listening to "the consumer message" and getting their act together so that we, as consumers, no longer have to suffer at the pump (as much) just because we don't want to manually shift our own transmission gears while driving!

Finally, if you're a Road Warrior Princess who enjoys the lap of luxury during some driving experiences while demanding 100% control for those more serious, strenuous, scary, or fuel-critical moments on the road, the semi-automatic transmission (also known as a clutchless manual transmission) was developed in Europe and is one of the best "middle-ground" solutions for your fuel economy needs. This unique transmission gives you control over how much fuel you are using, much like with a manual transmission, while also providing you the freedom you desire with an automatic transmission so you don't have to worry about the laborious exercise routine required of a stick shift while constantly engaging and disengaging the clutch during heavy traffic driving conditions!

Personally, I highly recommend this solution! I once had a little convertible car with a semi-automatic transmission in it and I absolutely loved driving it! So, get out there and go give your favorite make or model of car with a semi-automatic transmission in it a whirl and see how well you like it!

More Tips, Tricks, and Advice for "The Way You Drive"

Braking – As I mentioned earlier, your braking habits while driving can significantly increase the amount of fuel used when driving around town or even out on the Open Road! To avoid diminishing your MPG rating in between tanks, consider slowing down with plenty of time before red lights and literally "creeping up" to a slow rolled stop. Now, there are many Hypermilers (people who practice the use of driving techniques to maximize fuel economy) speaking out on the Internet, and advising that if you really want to achieve that "100 miles per gallon rating" between fuel ups at the pump, then you should never even tap the brakes on your car (not even at a stop sign).

However, as a Safety Conscious Road Warrior Princess, I strongly advise *against* making the "California Roll" (a driving practice of merely slowing down to a crawl but never actually stopping at red lights and stop signs) a regular driving habit, no matter how much you want to improve your MPG! Not only is this driving practice's legalities questionable, but it can also create confusion amongst other drivers traveling on the road around you. This confusion can oftentimes create a situation where, because of this driving practice, your Road Warrior Adventure may find itself in serious jeopardy of coming to a crashing halt, and that's just no fun any way you think about it! However, letting off the accelerator and slowly creeping up to the stop sign or stoplight without touching the brakes – this is PERFECTLY ACCEPTABLE when trying to get more bang for your buck out of each and every tank!

Additionally, for those of you Road Warriors driving a manual or semi-automatic transmission, "slowing down" and "stopping" situations are when you will enjoy the benefits of your choice in transmission the most. This is because, instead of repeatedly tapping on the brakes (such as you have to do with a typical automatic transmission), all you have to do when slowing down or stopping with these other transmission types is to just *gradually* shift down through the gears as your engine's RPM drop – and the transmission does the work of slowing down the vehicle instead of the brakes.

The added benefit of this driving practice, is that by *gradually slowing down* by shifting down through the gears, instead of engaging the brakes on your vehicle, your MPG can also improve – because oftentimes the traffic light will change to green by the time you get slowed down, so then it doesn't take much of a surge in RPM (or fuel and power usage) to shift your vehicle back into the proper gear and slowly (gracefully) *ease* back onto the accelerator to "get-going" down the road again. After all, it is the "hitting the gas" habit of most drivers that tends to make an engine work harder (and use more fuel). Anytime you can do something to adjust your driving habits to better regulate your speed and the RPM of your engine so that you can *ease* into a stop or *ease* back into an acceleration, you will likely use less energy (fuel) to get to where you are going!

Stop-and-Go Traffic – On the topic of easing in and out of accelerations while cruising down the road…the ever-ugly beast of bumper-to-bumper stop-and-go traffic is pretty much thought of as: 1) unavoidable; and 2) the death to fuel-efficiency! To better help you improve your miles per gallon (MPG), even under the most annoying of heavy traffic driving situations, try the following simple tricks:

1) Always leave a big space between your car and the car ahead of you;

2) Resist the urge to constantly tap on the brakes (instead, use your transmission gears to adjust your driving speed);

3) Simply allow the car to *slowly continue rolling* down the road as traffic moves along without hitting the accelerator.

So what happens when every opportunistic driver keeps cutting in front of you because you are leaving such a big space between your car and the next car ahead of you? Simple, do nothing, maintain your rolling speed and if they're in *that* much of a hurry, they'll be way ahead of you in no time flat! It's okay. You're still in control of your vehicle and cruising along at your optimal speed for best miles per gallon (and saving money), so just smile as you think of how much more money that other driver is spending on fuel than you because of their erratic driving habits and that should keep you calm and happy! However, if entertaining *that* thought *doesn't* make you smile, turn on your favorite music and "scream-sing" all that frustration out of your system!

Sitting at an Idle – Sometimes you just can't avoid it – You're sitting at an idle and all you can think is, "How much gas am I wasting just sitting here like this?" Now, if you're thinking at this point that you *shouldn't* turn off your engine because it's just going to make you use up *even more gas* to start the engine back up once it's time to get rolling again, in the age of modern Road Warrior Vehicles this assumption about fuel-efficiency isn't necessarily true anymore.

It appears to be the consensus of many Hypermilers that if your car is a relatively newer model vehicle, and you have been sitting idle for at least 10 seconds, then it is in your fuel tank's best interest for you to turn off the engine at that point. These claims suggest that *it actually requires less fuel* to restart the engine than it does to sit with the engine running idle for longer than 10 seconds – and now that I've said this, as of the writing of this book I have not seen any empirical scientific data either proving or disproving this theory. However, I do know that over the years I have noticed improvements in my MPG by utilizing this technique, so I'm passing it along to all those who would dare to find new simple solutions for helping our world's major energy crisis!

Take Advantage of the Driving Terrain – I truly believe that the Open Road is always sending us little "MPG Gifts" as we venture along the great paved highways of our life (the real ones) and it is up to every Astute Road Warrior Princess to take full advantage of these little driving terrain gifts as she travels along the path of her journey. Whether you're driving to and from work or hitting the great super highway for a week long Road Warrior Adventure – Every great downhill rush or small/slight decline along the map's path is an opportunity for you to use less fuel. So when you find yourself rolling down even the "teensiest" little decline in the road's elevation, give yourself permission to keep a few drops of fuel in your tank and lay off the accelerator so that gravity can do the work instead of your engine! Given enough of these little "MPG Gift" moments while cherishing the Open Road, you will easily find that you now have a few extra miles of fuel in your tank!

Cruise Control is Your Greatest Ally – Whether you have a "lead foot" or dazzle your Road Warrior Vehicle's accelerator with "featherweight" grace, the harsh reality is that no matter how skilled you are at regulating the accelerator, your car's cruise control accelerating button (also known as "Speed Control" or "Autocruise") can increase your acceleration in smaller increments than your foot ever will - while dramatically reducing your fuel consumption during longer journeys. If you have this feature on your Road Warrior Vehicle, use it! However, if you don't have the cruise control feature on your current vehicle, consider adding this feature during your next auto purchase! It's a great MPG improvement resource!

Adhere to the Posted Speed Limit – Not only is this Simple Rule for Road Warrior Princess SAFETY – It is also a heck of a good way to improve your miles per gallon (MPG)! So if you have the option of cruising down the freeway where you can maintain the posted speed limit in the right lane of the freeway (as oppose to traveling in the far left (passing) lane so you can breeze pass by all of those other "slow" drivers) - save yourself a little extra money per gallon by joining the "slow" drivers traveling at the *posted* speed limit in the far right-hand lane. (*For right-hand side road driving countries only, and for left side road driving countries – same advice, only other side of the lane!*) You will love the extra cashola in your wallet!

Weight Management 101 – As women, we know the joys (and pains) of watching our body weight, but when it comes to saving money at the pump and improving fuel economy, your Road Warrior Vehicle needs to watch its weight as well! According to sources on the Internet, guesstimates indicate that an extra 100 pounds of weight can hinder your MPG by as much as 1 to 2%. If you have extra books, magazines, groceries, shoe collections, or any other random (non-essential) baggage riding around with you in your car, clean it out and this can help improve your fuel-efficiency.

In addition to cleaning out the inside of your Road Warrior Vehicle, consider other weight reduction techniques, such as removing aftermarket trailer tow bars mounted on the underside of the rear bumper, as well as, any sports utility or luggage racks mounted on the roof of your vehicle.

After all, if you are not currently pulling a moving trailer or your favorite sport is not in season (so you have no need to use the roof rack), remove these heavy aftermarket vehicle accessories when they are not in use. Not only does removing aftermarket tow bars and roof racks *reduce* the amount of drag (wind resistance) created while traveling down the road (which improves fuel economy), but the reduction in weight can also improve the amount of miles you drive before returning to the fuel pump!

Go the Distance First – When planning your daily errands run, or merely planning to make various stops around town for a weekend of shopping, always drive to the furthest destination point on your to-do list first so that the engine has time to warm up and then work your way back home (or your final longest-term parking destination) from there. This is a Simple Rule to improve fuel-efficiency because your car or SUV's engine runs more efficiently and tends to use less fuel when stopping and starting after the engine has already been given a fair amount of distance driving to help it *really* warm up first.

3-Point Parking – Since we're on the topic of allowing the car engine to warm up for greater fuel-efficiency before conducting a lot of stopping and starting maneuvers. Another great way to reduce fuel consumption is by parking "face-out". If you plan on pulling into a parking lot where your vehicle's engine will have enough time to cool off before returning to your vehicle to leave the parking lot - Always try to park with the front of your Road Warrior Vehicle facing out so you can simply pull out of the parking space and go! This will eliminate the need to use extra fuel by having a cold engine perform a 3-point turn in order to back out of the parking space before leaving the parking lot.

A Word of Warning: When parking "face-out" double check the parking lot for posted signs prohibiting this parking practice because there are a lot of privately owned parking lots that do not allow vehicles to park this way in their parking lots. It would be unfortunate to have your car towed for not following the rules just because you're trying to save a couple of dollars on gas. Not to mention, it would defeat the purpose of trying to save a little money by parking "face-out" in the first place!

Drafting Larger Vehicles – I seriously questioned whether or not to even put this driving technique in this book. The thing is, if I don't, you're going to find out about it anyway, and much like a parent talking to kids about bad habits they can pick up at school – the reality is – it's just better for us to chat about this incredibly "MPG Boosting", yet EXTREMELY DANGEROUS *Way of Driving!*

What is "Drafting"?

Drafting Defined – Drafting (also commonly referred to as "tailgating" "riding 'their' bumper" and a variety of other terms and phrases, some not entirely appropriate for this book), is essentially the driving technique where a vehicle pulls up incredibly close behind the vehicle ahead of it (*less* than the travel distance in 2 seconds, or equivalently, one vehicle length for every 5 mph (8 km/h) of current speed) as a means of fuel and power conservation.

When the two vehicles are driving with very little space between the rear bumper of the first car and the front bumper of the second car - the cars are essentially able to split the wind resistance between them. This creates a situation where the vehicle driving in front of the rear vehicle is taking on the burden of cutting through the majority of the wind resistance (which requires more engine power and fuel usage) and the car in the back gets to basically "coast along" while the vehicle in front does all of the hard work for it.

The benefit of being the vehicle in the back of this type of driving duo is that you don't have to use *near* the engine power (nor the fuel) to achieve the same driving speed as the vehicle ahead that is being drafted. This is why the drafting technique is so favored by Hypermilers for conserving gas and engine power - because oftentimes, the drafting drivers receive an improved performance out of their vehicles for *essentially* a "discounted" fuel cost.

Road Warrior Tip: This form of tailgating (drafting) is also sometimes referred to as "slipstreaming". Alternatively, when the drafting vehicle TURNS OFF their engine while following the lead vehicle (which is EVEN MORE DANGEROUS to do because you can lose control of many of the "powered" safety features on your vehicle by turning off the engine: brakes, steering, etc.), it is called "draft-assisted forced stop" or "draft-assisted forced auto-stop" (D-FAS).

Why is it Dangerous?

Lack of Control – Although you may be benefitting from the joys of watching your gas gauge stay on "full" for longer than usual, the downside of this driving technique is that when you are the second car (the "Drafter") you have pretty much given up ALL CONTROL over your safety to another vehicle. Your driving safety is now in the hands of the front driver because you are stuck in the front vehicle's draft with no way of seeing what is "really" happening further down the road ahead of you.

It is often said that there are no free rides in this world, and in the case of drafting, the same holds true – only in the case of drafting, the price you pay for getting a higher MPG out of your tank is that you put yourself and your vehicle's safety at the mercy of a stranger's driving abilities. You also *give up* the ability to perform lifesaving emergency steering maneuvers with adequate reaction time.

Not to mention, when drafting, you exponentially increase the chances of being involved in a far more serious auto accident because of the *severity* of the dangers created by placing both your life and the lives of others at risk when performing this driving practice.

The dangers can be visualized when thinking about news reports we've all seen, read, or heard about from time to time – These dangers are the stories where you hear about an auto accident that results in one of the drivers being "decapitated" because he or she was drafting a much larger tractor-trailer type vehicle, such as an 18-wheel truck.

The tragedy strikes when a driver who is drafting a larger vehicle starts feeling "too comfortable" behind the wheel of their vehicle because they are *leisurely* being "pulled" along down the road by the larger vehicle's draft. Thus, the driver in the second car (the person drafting) stops paying attention to the road or the larger vehicle or truck ahead of it.

Consequently, when the vehicle ahead of this smaller drafting vehicle comes upon a driving situation on the road that requires the front vehicle to quickly come to a screeching stop, the driver in the second vehicle has very little, if any, warning.

Inevitably, the smaller vehicle drafting behind the larger truck doesn't have adequate driving reaction time to stop their vehicle before slamming into the rear of the vehicle ahead of it, which in these instances is typically the back of the trailer that the big truck is pulling.

As one might imagine, it is because of this *lack of reaction time* created by the limited space between the two vehicles that is required of a *true* drafting situation that ultimately leads to these gory decapitation accidents - such as heads being severed unnaturally from the drafting driver's body when their vehicle collides with the rear-end of a tractor-trailer truck. The sad reality is that these accidents truly do happen. These are not just scary stories they tell in driver's education classes; these are the cold harsh realities and dangers of following WAY TOO CLOSE behind a larger vehicle ahead of you just so you can enjoy the benefits of better gas mileage.

Now, I know the telling of such stories might sound a bit gruesome, but so are the realities and the dangers of practicing drafting as a driving technique just to save a few bucks on your fuel expenses. So, when it comes to such a serious and potentially life threatening topic – it is far better to understand the dangers of this driving practice by reading about it in this book than it is to experience the dangers firsthand (because you may not live to talk about it later)!

Legalities – Last, but not least, because of the growing frenzy to Hypermile your way into a higher MPG bracket across America, the authorities are on high alert to reduce dangers on the Open Road. If you are caught by the authorities driving as a "drafter" (by not leaving enough room between you and the vehicle ahead of you) you may just find yourself also being asked to give up control of some of your travel funds because drafting in the strictest sense of this driving technique is majoratively illegal (and with good reason).

Now, although I haven't cross-referenced this statement with every single traffic law for every road in the United States (or other countries) before stating that this is a "majoratively illegal" driving practice – Of which, I certainly recommend you check with your local motor vehicles department before taking this statement as fact - For the most part, it is safe to say that drafting, by definition, is typically considered a traffic violation on many roads in the United States that are accessible to the general driving public.

Ultimately, the dangers you encounter and the freedom you give up by drafting are not only control over your safety, your vehicle, the control that comes from having adequate driving reaction time behind the wheel of your car, and the ability to maneuver your vehicle safely out of harm's way during dangerous or unexpected driving conditions; the dangers of drafting also include the freedom you give up due to possibly being asked to hand over some of your hard-earned traveling funds to pay a traffic violation ticket or make a court summons appearance. Not to mention, the potential legal civil suit liability issues you may encounter should *your* drafting driving practices have created a real "mess" or harmed others while out on the Open Road - and that's just NO FUN!

So Why Do People Recommend "Drafting" for Improving MPG?

You've seen it in the movies and if you have ever been in a car while driving down the freeway, you have, most likely, already experienced it for yourself, to a greater or lesser degree. The truth is, sheer laws of physics create variations of drafting, in one form or another, regardless of whether or not you are conscientiously trying to draft another vehicle. As such, drafting has always been an influence on driving habits when it comes to the rules of the Open Road.
    Although various driving industries (auto racing, truck driving, etc.) have been taking advantage of the benefits of drafting for years (and experienced the downsides too) - More recently, "Hypermiling Mania" has brought this driving technique into the forefront of mainstream media for all to ponder, test, try, debate, and ultimately decide where their moral compasses stand on such a dangerous practice when utilized to extremes (such as with D-FAS).
    The truth is, that although the very worst you can imagine has and does result from practicing drafting driving techniques in its most dangerous practice, alternatively, drafting can equally be used as a survival technique for gas starved engines under both dire

circumstances and extreme Road Warrior Adventure driving conditions. The deliberation is whether the circumstances and risks of doing such outweigh the consequences by using this technique to save a few bucks on gas during your travels.

So this begs the question: Are there any driving situations when drafting may become a necessary option for a Road Warrior Princess while embracing her Open Road Adventures?

Absolutely!

Case in Point - Extreme Situations…

Road Warrior Story - It was a long dark night…I was driving down I-90, crossing the Great Plains of South Dakota in the midst of a cold chilling winter's night. My eyes were growing heavy from staring into the spotlight of night while looking down the Long Open Road, when it suddenly surprised me that I'd just missed my turnoff for gas on the freeway! Looking down at my fuel gauge, there was all of a quarter of a tank of gas left. Knowing my car as I did, that meant I'd be out of gas in approximately another 30 miles or so. "Where was I – and how far until the next gas station?" I wondered. There was nobody else on the road that night except for myself and the wildlife hiding in the shadows beyond the headlights outlining the sides of the road. It was official – I was scared. "What to do? What to do?"

Just then, my gift of a drafting opportunity came swooping in to save me. No sooner than the endless thoughts of all the varying ways this night could possibly turn *horribly wrong* and were plaguing my every minute, a big beautiful large truck with its 18-wheels of drafting power came flying pass by me and pulled right up in front of my little car. Soon after, a road sign read that the next town was 54 miles away. "I'm never going to make it!" I screamed silently to my inner self.

The truck was there… and so was I. 54 miles. 54 long miles. I could hear my own inner frantic thoughts whispering in my head, "Sure, Deb! Draft him!"

Road Warrior Tip: Now the trick about drafting, and the downside of drafting, is that there is this "very small" space of drafting opportunity between you and the vehicle ahead of you when attempted with "safety" in mind. Ultimately, the draft falling off the back of the vehicle ahead of you creates just enough space for you to benefit from the draft falling off of the larger vehicle ahead of you, but if you fall back too far, you get hit with a gushing wall of wind that slows you down. Alternatively, if you creep up too close, the draft can suck your vehicle in very close to the vehicle ahead of you, creating a situation where you then find yourself possibly feeling out of control or "too close" to the vehicle ahead of you. It also means that the vehicle or truck ahead of you may no longer be able to see you at all either. In this situation of feeling "too close", this is when you might ultimately be putting your own life and the lives of others at risk (as could have been my case, were there actually anybody else around that night).

Road Warrior Story Continues - Keeping this tip in mind, I pulled up to the "sweet spot" (somewhere in between "too close" and "not close enough" for it to be useful to follow this truck) so that my vehicle was just as close as I felt safe doing so and just until I could feel my car "give in" a little to the draft coming off of the larger truck ahead of me – and whoosh! We were off!

As we were cruising along, my gas gauge barely moved and I was loving the "pull along" I was receiving from this truck as we cruised together under the night sky down the freeway – BUT! Here's the problem with drafting. Simply put – it is far too easy to get "too comfortable" behind the wheel when a larger vehicle is "pulling" you along down the road. In fact, it's *downright scary* how easy it is to grow far *too comfortable* behind the wheel when it isn't taking much effort to navigate your Road Warrior Vehicle behind a much larger vehicle that is pulling your car down the road. I say it's scary because it's easy to just flat-out no longer pay attention to the road when another vehicle is doing the work for your car – it's like being a passenger in somebody else's car, only from within and behind the wheel of your own car (were that even possible).

Simple Statement About <u>WHY I DON'T</u> Condone this Driving Practice …Not by Any Stretch of the Imagination!

Road Warrior Tip: Should you lose control of your vehicle in the whipping winds created by the draft; or for one second become too comfortable enjoying the "pull" down the road by another larger vehicle; or you take your eyes off of what the vehicle ahead of you is doing while leisurely being pulled down the road - You may find yourself frantically faced with a situation where it becomes difficult to get back in sync with the vehicle ahead of you due to whipping winds or other unforeseen driving circumstances. This is because, in order for the strictest definition of the drafting technique to *truly work*, the second vehicle has to follow the front vehicle's every move. Needless to say, my first thoughts regarding this experience of feeling as though I was possibly losing or could easily lose control of my own vehicle while attempting to "safely" draft this truck was that this feeling of getting *far too comfortable behind the wheel* after so many miles could possibly create a VERY DANGEROUS situation. After feeling this way, that was it for me! No more "trying out" drafting!

Road Warrior Story Continues – I did make it to my next fuel stop safe and sound that night, but in hindsight (and with the blessing of that hindsight being 20/20 while still alive to tell the story) - This Road Warrior Experience in and of itself scared the *ever-lovin' begeebers* out of me!

So, even if drafting does get a thumbs up by many Hypermilers, and in spite of the fact that it did get me to the next gas station that night - *It is NOT on my list of "The Top Ways of Driving to Save a Few Bucks Between Fuel Ups at the Pump"…for <u>Safety</u> Reasons!* However, the rest of these tips are…

Keep that Air Conditioning Turned Off! – The truth is…the weather has a large influence on just how much energy your engine requires to carry you down the Open Road (and how much fuel usage). One of the biggest gas-guzzling features on your vehicle is the air conditioner. Although this feature can serve as a fantastic survival tool when driving under varying weather conditions, it is also a primary MPG killer! Simple Rule – If you don't need the air conditioner, keep it turned off! Your fuel-efficiency can dramatically improve!

In Daylight Leave "Day" Lights Turned Off – Most newer Road Warrior Vehicles have built-in safety features, such as automatic running daylight headlights. This is great for safety, but horrible for fuel-efficiency. If you can safely drive without your headlights on, turn those bad-boys off until just before sundown and save yourself a few drops of gas!

Headwinds and Crosswinds Can Defeat Your Best Efforts – The cold harsh reality is that no matter how careful you are about *the way you drive*, if you're driving into a strong headwind or consistently driving across wide open plains that have strong crosswind weather patterns along these roads, then your MPG could end up dropping like a *Bear Stock Market* and your wallet is going to take the brunt of the burden in fuel expenses!

To avoid such defeatist driving situations, the best course of action is to plan your driving routes more effectively so you are consistently driving roads that either: 1) place the wind behind your vehicle so it creates a tailwind that will help push you down the road; and/or 2) plan your driving course so that you are primarily driving down roads that are heavily lined with various trees and shrubbery to block the wind from swooshing across the road. These two tips can help you dramatically reduce the amount of wind resistance your Road Warrior Vehicle encounters when traveling, and thus, can reduce the amount of work your engine has to do so you can enjoy the benefits of greatly improved fuel-efficiency!

While we're on the topic of extending your fuel-efficiency: What should you do if you run out of gas? This question leads us to our next series of Simple Rules for the Road Warrior Princess…

Simple Rule 7

In Case Of Emergency - Don't Panic!

A Road Warrior Princess Is

Always Prepared!

Rule #7 – In Case of Emergency – Don't Panic!

A Road Warrior Princess is *Always Prepared* to deal with any situation that may come her way while out on the Open Road!

First, I'd like to mention that there are a plethora of roadside assistance programs out there. Some are offered when you purchase your vehicle directly from an auto dealership, while others are offered through privately held or publicly held companies that serve only this purpose. Alternatively, certain auto insurance providers and credit card companies also offer a variety of roadside assistance programs. Regardless of where you purchase your roadside assistance program, if you have one, this is a great resource for the Die-hard Road Warrior Princess.

However, if you are running on say, a "thinner budget" than others and cannot afford the subscription dues associated with a roadside assistance program, consider this book your roadside assistant when traveling! It outlines just about everything you will need to know should you find yourself in a situation that doesn't require a call to your auto insurance provider (of which, you should have one of these too)!

What To Do If You Run Out of Fuel

The first thing to know about your car is that your fuel gauge is very rarely 100% accurate. Keep this in mind at ALL TIMES when out on the Open Road. Second, the best answer for what to do if you run out of gas is - Don't let yourself run out of gas!

A Simple Rule to follow for ensuring that you never run out of gas when traveling is to fuel up every time your vehicle's fuel gauge drops below the half mark and is just above the quarter of a tank mark on the fuel gauge. Although this statement hasn't been scientifically tested, it seems to me that oftentimes the upper half of the tank appears to last longer than the bottom half of the tank. Case in Point - Have you ever noticed that your fuel gauge seems to stay above the half tank mark for sometimes 200+ miles, but then the gas warning light comes on after you go another 70 or 80 miles once the gauge indicates there is only a half a tank left? Although it may be different MPG ratings for various makes and models of vehicles, the point is still the same - The bottom half of the tank just never seems to last as long as the top half of the tank. So remember this and always fuel up when you're getting closer to hitting that quarter of a tank mark to prevent running out of fuel in the first place! However...

When Might a Road Warrior Princess Run Out of Gas?

Under a variety of unforeseen circumstances, there are still times when the Road Warrior Princess might run out of gas, such as:

- When you are driving faster than normal (say across the states of South Dakota, Wyoming, and Montana going 75+ miles per hour) while driving straight into a hard headwind, which is not uncommon for these areas of the nation, or just driving into a hard wind for an extensive period of time (regardless of driving speed).
- When you are driving up a long and torturously steep mountain grade, and your vehicle winds up using more fuel to climb those hills than you had previously thought it would.
- If you are pulling a trailer, such as a moving trailer, behind your vehicle - This can cut your normal gas mileage almost in half of what you're use to getting when driving without a trailer hitched to the rear bumper.
- Sitting idle with the engine running for an extensive period of time, such as when stuck in a traffic jam because of road construction or leaving the engine running while resting.
- Excessively exceeding the legal speed limit - Aside from this driving practice being considered especially risky to your

health and safety, excessively exceeding the legal posted speed limit just kills your gas mileage every time!
- Driving in rough terrain, on rough roads, or in *really bad* weather where your tires are constantly slipping and sliding, or where you are unable to maintain a steady speed due to driving conditions.
- Driving long distances with the air conditioner turned on in your Road Warrior Vehicle.

These are just a few of the many reasons for why you might suddenly not get as good of gas mileage as you thought you would, and thus might run out of gas.

The good news is that due to this country rapidly becoming populated, anymore, there are usually gas stations within 30–80 miles of each other, even in remote states like South Dakota, where 10-15 years ago (as of the writing of this book), this wasn't the case. Back then, if you didn't strategically plan your fuel stops while driving through South Dakota, there was a good chance you'd run out of gas. Now, gas stations seem to be everywhere!

However, if you do run out of gas, there is a product on the market that I always keep in the trunk of my car for just such a miserable occasion. Although there are various brand names for it on the open market, it is typically referred to as an Emergency Fuel Additive. You can purchase a bottle of it at just about any automotive store in the country or online. This product can get you down the road sometimes another 2-3 miles, which depending on where you have run out of gas, it can at least keep your car going until reaching a nearby gas station to refuel.

What To Do If Your Car Starts To Overheat

There are many reasons for why a car with a perfectly good thermostat could start to overheat while cruising down the Open Road during your Die-hard Road Warrior Princess Adventure. Here are some of the most common:

Possible Overheating Problem #1 - You forgot to check the radiator's coolant reserve container to make sure there is still enough coolant (antifreeze) in your car and now it is empty, causing your car to overheat.

Solution: *With the engine turned off,* pour more coolant (antifreeze) in the radiator's coolant reserve container, which is usually located NEXT to the actual radiator under the hood toward the front of your vehicle's engine (refer to your vehicle owner's manual for exact location).

A Word of Warning: Never pour coolant (antifreeze), water, or any liquids directly into your radiator!!! If a radiator cap is taken off, even after a few hours of the engine running and then being turned off, the scolding hot radiator fluid can spew out of the radiator and land on you, burning you terribly. This is not a good thing to have happen to you on your Road Warrior Princess Adventure!

Second, even if the car's engine hasn't run in days, ***DO NOT POUR COOLANT, ANTIFREEZE, WATER, OR ANY OTHER LIQUID DIRECTLY INTO YOUR RADIATOR*** - Doing this can also damage your radiator or cooling system! Again, not a good way to spend your Road Warrior Princess Adventure!

Road Warrior Tip: If you do not have access to antifreeze or coolant and cannot get to a service station to purchase this item, pull out your bottle of water or quart of water from the trunk of your vehicle and fill the radiator's coolant reserve container to the "MAX" Line with water.

A Word of Warning: Be cautious about adding water during freezing or cold winter weather months to prevent creating potentially damaging effects to your cooling system. The water poured in the radiator's coolant reserve container may freeze if the weather gets too cold while the engine is off.

Solution Continued: Next, allow the car to rest for about a half an hour until the engine can cool down. Then, see if the engine will start back up again and the temperature stabilizes after having waited for a little while.

Once your car engine is started, let it run for a few minutes, then turn off the engine, pop the hood open and check the radiator's coolant reserve container level again. You may notice that the radiator's coolant reserve container liquid level is now lower than where it was after you first filled it up to the "MAX" Line. If the liquid level is

SIMPLE RULE 7: IN CASE OF EMERGENCY – DON'T PANIC!

closer to the "MIN" Line than the "MAX" Line again, add more coolant (antifreeze) or water until the liquid level in the radiator's coolant reserve container is back at the "MAX" Line.

Repeat this process of filling the radiator's coolant reserve container to the "MAX" Line, putting the lid back on the radiator's coolant reserve container, then after each filling, start the engine, let it run for a few minutes, then turn the engine off, and check the radiator's coolant reserve container liquid line level over and over again until the liquid level finally stays close to the "MAX" Line in the radiator's coolant reserve container after the engine is turned off.

If your car was overheating, chances are the radiator will need to pull more coolant (antifreeze) or water from the coolant reserve container back into the radiator (which is done when the engine is turned on) to help fill up the radiator and balance things out so that the cooling system works properly again. You will know that you have replaced the proper amount of coolant (antifreeze) or water in your radiator once you can turn on and off the engine and the liquid level in the radiator's coolant reserve container *stays* closer to the "MAX" Line.

Finally, make sure the radiator's coolant reserve container cap is tightly placed back on the container before starting the engine (as it should be EVERY TIME the engine is running, or hot liquid can spray all over the place), and return to your Road Warrior Adventure!

If you continue to notice your car overheating for no apparent reason after this first overheating incident, please make sure you get your car's thermostat tested, and possibly replaced, at the nearest auto service station in the next town. This is a relatively inexpensive auto part at most auto parts stores (plus the cost of labor to replace the part). However, replacing the thermostat in your Road Warrior Vehicle can typically resolve most any overheating problems when traveling the Open Road!

Possible Overheating Problem #2 - You are driving up a steep grade under the hot blazing sun (such as down I-5 just northeast of Los Angeles, California) and you have the air conditioning in your vehicle turned to its coolest setting with the fan on the highest setting.

Solution: As much as you will hate this solution, I highly recommend it because I have seen everybody from people with really old beaten up cars, to brand new limos broken down on the side of the road because they drove up a steep grade or hill with the air conditioner on when it was blistering hot outside.

The solution to this problem is to TURN OFF your vehicle's air conditioner, ROLL DOWN your windows, and TURN ON the heater to the hottest setting with the heater fan on the highest setting to blow out all of the hot air trapped under the engine hood of your car. Continue to keep the heater fan on high while going up these steep hills, or until the heat gauge indicates that your engine has cooled off enough to be considered back within reasonable heat levels for your make and model of Road Warrior Vehicle. However, just because your engine cools back off after running the heater to release all of that hot air under the hood - DO NOT turn the air conditioner back on once the engine has cooled. Instead, turn off the heater fan and continue to drive with the windows rolled down to keep yourself cooled off until arriving at the nearest auto service center where you can then have your vehicle's cooling system checked out by a professional (or, if overheating is due to being low on coolant - someplace where you can add more coolant to the radiator's coolant reserve container yourself).

I know this sounds miserable - and hot - and sweaty, but better to suffer for possibly only 5-10 minutes while pulling a steep grade, than to suffer for 3-4 hours under the blazing hot sun while waiting for a tow truck!

Road Warrior Tip: To be honest with you, when I'm traveling anywhere in the country under these types of hot weather conditions - whether towing a trailer up a steep hill, driving across the desert under the blazing hot sun, or pulling a forever long grade on a hot day (with or without a trailer), I don't even wait to see if my gauges start reading that my car is getting hot. As soon as I recognize a potential overheating situation on the Open Road, I just automatically turn off the air conditioner, roll down the car windows, and turn my car's heater fan on HIGH so there is absolutely NO RISK (or at least, VERY LITTLE risk) of overheating my car's engine.

Although this may sound a little presumptuous, the sad thing about overheating your car is that if you ever overheat your vehicle's engine once, or if you even let it start "getting hot" once, you can have overheating problems with your car until you either: 1) get rid of the car; or 2) get the problem fixed. For whatever reason, it seems like automobile engines are just never the same after you overheat them that first time. It's as though you have now somehow traumatized your car for life!

Possible Overheating Problem #3 - Your thermostat isn't working properly and you may need to have it replaced, *or* you may have another part in your cooling system that is not functioning properly and you need to have your car serviced and have other possible cooling system parts repaired or replaced.

Solution: Have your Road Warrior Vehicle's thermostat replaced at the nearest service station in the next town. This is a relatively inexpensive auto part to replace at most auto parts stores (plus the cost of labor to replace the part). If the thermostat is not the problem, please make sure that the problem is discovered by the auto service center technician and that any parts that need to be replaced or repaired are *completely* replaced or repaired at that time. As always, be sure to ask the technician who is servicing your vehicle how any parts that need to be repaired or replaced are suppose to work - and ask to see with your own eyes how it is that *this* technician *knows* that YOUR PART is *not* working! Remember, a Road Warrior Princess is just as smart, if not more intelligent than the mechanic!

What To Do If You Get a Flat Tire

Sometimes it just happens. One minute you're cruising down the Open Road singing your favorite song to the radio or stereo at the top of your lungs, and the next you've turned off the music and are doing the best you can to control the steering wheel, slow down, and pull over to the side of the road, safely, due to a wobbling tire.
    The biggest question I'm usually faced with when this happens is, "Exactly how much further can I drive before I absolutely *have to* pull over?" And - I'll admit it…Depending on where I'm at in the country, I've been known to push my luck from time to time just so I can get to a safe rest area, or pull off the road down an off-ramp that is near a gas station, because to be quite honest; I hate being stranded on the side of the road!
    However, if you're familiar with the area or know that you are in a relatively safe location, you should immediately pull over to the side of the road (double-checking that your car is parked a safe distance

away from the traffic lane) to avoid potentially warping the rim(s) of the affected wheel(s) due to the flat or wobbling tire(s). After all, purchasing a new tire is typically less expensive than purchasing a new wheel - especially trying to get one(s) that match the other wheels, no less - *and* still having to buy a new tire or tires.

Depending on your situation, sometimes the tire going flat while you're actually driving down the road can oftentimes be prevented with proper maintenance.

Every time, or at least every other time you stop for gas, check your tires. Sometimes, kicking them to make sure there is enough air in them isn't enough. Especially, if you've been driving through a lot of back country roads or industrial areas, you should get down to your tires' level and look at the tread on each of the tires to see if there are any nail or screw heads, shards of metal, glass, or any other potentially hazardous objects stuck to, or in, the tread of your tire (the tread is the part of the tire that touches the road as the wheel goes around).

Another way to suspect that your tire may have a problem is if every so often you have to fill up the same tire with air (say every 300 miles, or when driving around local areas, every week or two). An object puncturing the sidewall or tread of your tire, such as a nail or screw, can typically create a slow leak.

If you suspect one of your tires has a slow leak, or you see anything that looks like a nail or screw head stuck to your tire tread or sidewall, *do not attempt to pull it out yourself*, because doing this will most likely cause your tire to go flat in a matter of seconds. Instead, take your vehicle to the nearest tire service center, either in your home town BEFORE leaving for your Road Warrior Adventure, or if currently on your journey, the next town with a tire service center to have the tire inspected, the lodged item(s) removed from your tire, and have the tire patched (repaired) or replaced.

On a side note, even if taking time out of your travel plans to fix the problem *does slightly delay* your Road Warrior Adventure, it is still a lot less expensive, and a lot less time-consuming, to *prevent a blowout from happening* while out on the Open Road, than it is to try and keep your calm when you suddenly find yourself *with a flat tire* on the Open Road.

SIMPLE RULE 7: IN CASE OF EMERGENCY – DON'T PANIC!

What To Do Once Stranded by a Blowout or Wobbling Wheel or Tire?

Unfortunately, sometimes a blowout or a wobbling wheel or flat tire cannot be prevented while driving down the Open Road. In the event that this is your situation, never fear, you have a few options to get back on the Open Road safely (and in a somewhat timely fashion):

Solution #1: Call a tow truck and have them transport your vehicle back to the nearest tire service center to repair or replace the affected tire.

Solution #2: Call a tow truck and have somebody else remove the damaged wheel and/or flat tire and replace it with the donut (spare tire) located (usually) in the trunk's storage compartment.

Solution #3: Remove the damaged wheel and/or flat tire and replace it with the donut (spare tire) from your trunk yourself (sometimes you cannot get a cell phone signal to call for roadside assistance or a tow truck, so this is a good thing to know how to do on your own, if you ever need to do it yourself). After replacing the damaged tire with the spare tire (make sure all of the lug nuts are on as tight as you can get them), *slowly* drive to the next town with a tire service center and have the damaged tire replaced or repaired, balanced, and placed back on your vehicle.

Solution #4: Take a can of liquid inflator and sealant for your tires out of the trunk of your car and fill up the flat tire with the solution so that you may travel safely until reaching the next town to replace the damaged tire. Please note that when you fill up your tire using canned liquid products that are intended to inflate your tire *and* seal the leak, these products squeeze an oozy sticky-like substance *into* your tire. In order to repair the tire later, many repair shops will insist that you *must* replace the tire (because it's too difficult to clean out the tire so they can apply a patch, if necessary, once the product hardens inside your tire).

Road Warrior Tip: If you are unsure about how to use this product, *read the directions very carefully* and follow them. Overfilling the tire, or having other hazardous tire conditions existing when the product is applied to the tire, may cause further damage. (This statement is made on condition of speaking from personal experience only.)

What To Do If it is Slick or Snowy Outside and You Can't Get Going After Having Stopped on the Side of the Road

<u>OR</u>

What To Do If You Slide into a Ditch and the Tires on the Car Cannot Get Enough Traction to Get Going Again

To Answer BOTH Questions: If nobody is hurt from the car sliding off the road, and your car is not buried in a snowbank (this would require a tow truck), the following is an important item to carry with you during your travels, either inside the car or in the trunk of your car near the spare tire, depending on the time of year and the region of the country you are traveling:

A Small Bag of Kitty Litter – Whether you own a cat or not, the sandy grit of clumping or scoopable kitty litter is a great resource to have in your car when you're traveling during the winter months. Over the years, I have come to realize that a snowstorm can strike just about *any area* of the country at anytime – Mother Nature is weird like that.

If you get in a slick situation or slide off the road and can't get going again, just sprinkle a little kitty litter near the front and rear sections where each tire touches the ground (try to push the kitty litter as far *under* the tread of the tire as you can). It works like a charm to help your tires grip enough traction to get out of a "slippery" or "stuck" situation. You'll never be stuck in the snow or wind up relentlessly spinning your wheels on the ice again!

Keep in mind, that under extreme winter weather driving conditions, having tire chains to put on your tires is also a great item to keep in the trunk of your car. However, not everybody needs tire chains; sometimes just a little traction (kitty litter) to get going again is all it takes, so use each of these resources according to your current weather condition and driving situation.

What To Do If You Hear Your Car Making a Weird Noise While Driving Down the Road, <u>BUT</u> the Car Still Seems to Operate Okay

I can't even begin to count the number of times my car has suddenly started making a weird or strange noise while driving down the Open Road, yet my car didn't appear to have anything "functionally" wrong with it while I was driving.

In this strange situation, the best course of action for the Road Warrior Princess traveling the Open Road alone, is to turn down the music, assess the situation, and make sure all of your controls are working properly (steering, transmission, acceleration pedal, and brakes are the big ones). If everything appears to function okay, slow down a bit (while making sure to maintain good speed with the rest of the flow of traffic) to see if the weird or strange noise changes at all.

If there isn't any smoke or steam coming out from under the hood, or out of your engine (or any place else on the vehicle), and you can't readily recognize the problem while driving, proceed to the nearest town with a car service center or gas station with a mechanic to have the noise checked out by a professional.

Now, I know some people might say you should pull over immediately, but I say…not necessarily. In my experience, many strange noises tend to come about after either: 1) I've recently driven over debris on the road, such as a piece of metal or a plastic bag that decided to attach itself to the underside of my car; or 2) as a result of road or weather driving conditions. Examples include: when driving in really wet or rainy weather conditions and the water from the road builds up condensation inside the tailpipe of my exhaust system; or when small pebbles or rocks from the road get stuck inside the hubcap (wheel cover), which can also create some pretty petrifying "weird noises"!

Not surprisingly, no sooner than I've arrived at a gas station or auto service center, the noise was gone. Many times, once stopped, I could always discover where the noise was coming from and correct the problem myself without paying for services to have someone else figure it out for me (such as being able to dislodge a plastic bag making "weird noises" after it became stuck to the underside of my vehicle).

However, if you can't figure out the source of the weird or strange noise for yourself and you are really concerned about it, you should always have a professional auto technician advise you about the possible reasons for why there is a noise coming from your Road Warrior Vehicle.

Tips on How to Know When to Pull Over on the Side of the Road

In my opinion, a Road Warrior Princess should never put her own life at risk by pulling over to the side of a highway or freeway *unless* she is in clear and present danger (or when being hailed to do so by the authorities). I can't tell you how many times I've driven down the road only to see somebody out of their car on the side of the road, getting something out of the trunk or the back seat, when they were no more than 10 miles away from a safe place to pull over, such as a rest area or gas station. This sickens me because I know that these people are not thinking about, nor noticing, the way the other drivers passing them on the road are swerving and becoming chaotic in the lanes around them...and all because the other vehicle on the side of the road "just had to pull over on *the side* of the road" *instead* of holding out a little while longer so they could pull over, *away from high-speed traffic*, in the rest area or gas station not even 1-10 miles further down the road. To stress my point, cars and trucks speed down the highway, oftentimes at driving speeds exceeding 65 or even 75 miles per hour. Comparatively, *you* are one little human body (compared to these larger vehicles) and can easily become harmed when standing so close to high-speed traffic.

To further emphasize my point, out on the Open Road, there are many *huge* 18-wheel (also called tractor-trailer) trucks speeding down the road. Sometimes the weary drivers of these big rigs cannot even see that a car has pulled off to the side of the road until the last second, and oftentimes when these cars on the side of the road have pulled over, their vehicles were parked *way too close* to the traffic lane too. This can create a crisis situation for the drivers of these larger trucks (or any size vehicle, for that matter) because if a driver doesn't see a car parked on the side of the road until the last second, many times the driver may not have enough reaction time to get over into the passing lane or move away from the parked vehicle before passing it.

Not only does the driver passing the parked car become terrified of hurting the passengers of the parked car, but considering the wind gusts coming off of the freeway or highway traffic alone (regardless of vehicle size), this excessive thrusting force from the wind created by passing vehicles traveling down the road can be enough to throw a person standing on the side of the road off balance and into traffic or harm's way. Needless to say, sometimes pulling over during "non-emergency" situations is an excessive risk to take when out on the Open Road.

Not to mention, have you ever watched someone swerve a little off the road when the driver of the car is either drunk, tired, or just flat out not paying attention to what s/he is doing? How alert do you think these tired or inattentive travelers are to the fact that *you* have pulled over on the side of the road just so you can get something out of your trunk "real quick"? Not very alert - at best!

I have seen far too many unnecessary things happen to other people while traveling the Open Road. So, my advice to you when it comes to whether or not you should pull over to the side of the road or whether you should just try to hold out a little longer until you can safely pull off the road into a rest area or gas station to take care of any necessary tasks while traveling is this:

"Hold out for as long as you can (unless it's a critical emergency) – and if you can make it to a rest area or gas station before stopping the vehicle - Do it!"

Other people are not watching out for you in high-speed traffic areas if you decide to pull over to the side of the road; so take the safe approach and pull off the road where you won't be putting yourself and others in harm's way *when you do* pull over.

The Truth About

Truck Drivers And Large Trucks!

Rule #8 – The Truth About Truck Drivers and Large Trucks

You might be a Road Warrior Princess, but the Truck Drivers and "18-wheelers" unofficially rule the Open Road!

This Simple Rule is a hard pill to swallow for some drivers, but the reality is that if you're not driving a Bigger Truck than they are, you are not as big as they are, even if you *are* faster than they are when embracing the Open Road. So simply put, if you want to stay out of harm's way, you will need to respect the fact that these big rigs cruising down the highway have some serious issues to deal with that you may never know about.

Lessons I Learned from My Dad About Sharing the Open Road with Truckers

Dad's Truck Driver Lesson #1 - You are small and insignificant compared to those big trucks, so stay out of their way!

Dad's Truck Driver Lesson #2 - If you're going to pass a big truck, get out and get around them, as quick as possible.

How many times have you seen shredded bits of tire rubber lying in the middle, or along the side, of the road? When a big rig like an 18-wheeler (or as some call them, a semi or tractor-trailer truck) blow a tire, the air pressure from the tire blowing out can be enough to shatter your car window if you just happen to be idly hanging out next to the truck while driving down the road for miles on end. So if you have to pass a large truck, get out in the other lane to pass them, get around them, and get back into your lane or move pass them down the freeway.

Most important, make an effort to pass them without "dilly-dallying around" (as my father once put it)!

Dad's Truck Driver Lesson #3 - Big trucks pulling trailers have blind spots. If you follow too close to the rear end of a truck, (especially their rear right corner) the driver of that truck most likely cannot see you.

At night, a good rule of thumb is to think like a truck driver. If a truck is passing you and it looks like they're not sure how much further they have to pull forward before they can get back over into the right lane, flash your headlights one time for them, once they get far enough past you, to signal to the truck driver that they can safely move back over now. This helps them tremendously and as you travel down the road, the trucks will begin to understand that you respect them as travelers of the Open Road, and in return, they may start to watch out for you too as you travel along the Mighty Open Road.

This works really well in states like Pennsylvania where the roads are hilly and winding and the wind whips through the mountains in such a way that it creates gusts and drafts of wind that can sometimes make your vehicle feel slightly out of control (under certain driving conditions) because everything is moving so fast. So knowing you have others watching out for you is a great benefit to have on your side during just such a Road Warrior Adventure driving occasion!

Dad's Truck Driver Lesson #4 - I'd like to describe this lesson with a little story my dad once told me about an experience he had back when he use to drive logging trucks for a living:

Dad's Truck Driver Story - Once upon a time (as all good stories start out) my dad was driving his logging truck with a full load of timber logs loaded down on his trailer. He had quite a heavy load that day and had just started out on his journey to his delivery destination. Cruising along, he started to ease off the accelerator and began shifting down through the gears to slow down the heavy rig for a stoplight he could see further up ahead. Just then, an impatient driver in a much smaller vehicle decided to cut around his truck, pulled in front of him, and then proceeded to *slam* on the brakes in front of him, leaving my father with even less time to slow down his load-bearing truck. Now if my father had been driving a little car or even a pickup truck this wouldn't have been such a big deal; he could have just slammed on the brakes to avoid colliding with the other vehicle. However, when driving a loaded down big truck with many tons of weight pushing the truck forward while trying to slow the truck down, "stopping on a dime" isn't such an easy task.

Consequently, because of the other driver's ignorance or lack of respect for truck drivers, my father had a BIG decision to make in less than a handful of seconds. If he kept on the course he was headed, he would not be able to get his truck stopped in time and his BIG truck would have driven over the smaller vehicle that just pulled in front of him only to slam on its brakes. This decision possibly would've killed the driver of the other vehicle that just cut him off. His second option: he could dump his truck and his load of timber logs (in other words, ruin his truck and his present means of income) to save the life of that presumably rude driver.

My dad chose to save the life of the other driver by rapidly swerving off course and consequently throwing his truck off of a ledge down the side of the road because there was no other option or place for his truck to go other than to drive it down a steep hillside to the right of the road. My father was lucky; he didn't lose his life that day. However, what the other driver who cut in front of him (only to slam on the brakes) most likely didn't realize - was that *had* my father lost his life that day - it would have been in an effort to save the life of that other person. Furthermore, it would have been in spite of the fact that this other person was the one creating the situation which could have easily of taken their own life as well…had my dad not risked his own life – or made the split-second decision he made *the very second* he'd made it to steer his truck off-course and off the road to avoid such tragedies from happening to this other driver.

The moral of this story isn't to scare you if you are a truck driver. It is to make the little car or SUV driver aware of the tough choices truck drivers have to make between saving the lives of other people or saving their own – Especially when another driver does something inconsiderate and unintelligent out on the Open Road.

If you are unaware of the fact that it takes much longer for a larger truck hauling a load (a trailer) to stop or make various driving maneuvers than it does for a smaller car or SUV, these types of dangerous driving choices when traveling near large tractor-trailer trucks *does* and can kill you or the truck driver. Please remember this and give those truck drivers out on the Open Road enough room and time to slow down so that you don't have to be the one responsible for a trucker possibly losing his or her life or livelihood just to save yours.

A Final Note About Dad's Truck Driver Lessons…

The main reason I want to stress this point about my dad's truck driving story and "his" rules for the Open Road (where driving around large trucks is concerned) is because the phenomenon of smaller vehicles creating dangerous situations on the road when driving near or around larger tractor-trailer type trucks really does upset me. On the last road trip I took across the country I counted a total of seven large trucks flipped over on their sides off the side of the road. With further investigation, most of these trucks were lying on their sides because the drivers of these larger trucks chose to risk their *own* life and livelihood in order to save the life of a driver that would've wound up injured or dead due to his or her poor driving choices, had the truck driver *not* sacrificed themselves first for the other driver. Be Safe – Respect the Open Road Truck Driver!

Simple Rule 9

Maintain A Zen-like State Of Mind Behind The Wheel!

Rule #9 – Maintain a Zen-like State of Mind Behind the Wheel!

This is a basic survival technique I think everybody should learn - Not just for peace of mind, but because when you are calm, cool, and collected behind the wheel, you have a tendency to be more aware of your surroundings and make better driving decisions. This is the state of mind you must learn to master as a Road Warrior Princess!

For those of you who are wondering, no this is not a book on yoga or spiritual enlightenment, but knowing how to maintain a Zen-like "state of being" behind the wheel of a car is good advice for those extremely stressful and "test of will" moments that you are *almost guaranteed* to encounter when traveling out on the Open Road.

Zen 101 for the Road Warrior Princess

The following techniques work great for bringing the Zen-conscious Road Warrior Princess back to a calm and relaxed state of mind should you find yourself feeling nervous, jittery, overstressed, confused, or whenever your mind begins feeling chaotic while driving:

Maintain a Zen-like State of Mind Technique #1 - This first technique incorporates the situation where maybe you're cruising down the Open Road - You're singing your favorite song at the top of your lungs (hopefully you're one of the few fortunate souls to have a terrific singing voice…and even if you aren't - just remember we're all Super Stars when we're singing alone in the car!)…and you're cruising along, only to discover that suddenly the road is twisting and turning a little faster and a little tighter than you thought it would. Worst of all, you've suddenly found yourself trapped in the passing lane so you can't even get over to slow down because some guy with really big headlights and smiley face covers on his fog lights is RIGHT on your bumper behind you! In what feels like a situation with almost very little warning, you've now found yourself completely yanked out of your happy driving state of being and are now panicking! What do you do? What do you do?

In this situation, you really only have about two options:

- The first option: you can have a panic attack, lock your arms up so every turn is like cranking a rigid wheel around each curve in the road – "clunk – clank – jerk!"…And the entire experience leaves you feeling as though you may never want to get back out on the Open Road ever again, in your life!

- The second option is to have a little fun with your newfound situation!

In just such a circumstance, I like to pretend that I'm an Indy Race Car Driver. At this point, I push my torso back into my driver's seat, make sure my arms and wrists are in a slightly bent and relaxed, yet slightly firm controlling position, and then pretend that my body is "One" with the vehicle. If the car sways right, I allow my body to glide with it. I am "One" with my car and in complete control!

Road Warrior Story - One day, while driving through Montana, just as the freeway drops down the east side of Lookout Pass I decided to experiment with this little technique to see which technique made me feel more at ease. *Option one* - I just sit in the car and drive like I would be sitting if I were in the city or were on a long straight stretch of highway; or *Option two* - I visualize my body position becoming "One" with the car around every twist and turn of the road.

The results? I was more at ease, felt less tension in my arms, shoulders, and neck, and had *way more control* over the car when I visualized myself becoming "One" with the car, than when I felt like I was *just a driver* and I was steering *just my car* around every twist and turn in the road. So try this technique of visualizing yourself becoming "One" with your Road Warrior Vehicle the next time you find yourself driving through a series of twists and turns that scare you…I bet you'll find yourself becoming more calm, relaxed, and feel more in control of your vehicle. However, just because I feel obligated to say this, if you still feel out of control – SLOW DOWN! That guy with the smiley face covers on his fog lights will just have to deal!

Maintain a Zen-like State of Mind Technique #2 - Icy road conditions are by far one of the SCARIEST experiences when driving the Open Road, especially if you weren't expecting to deal with this situation on your road trip so you didn't prepare by putting the appropriate heavy duty winter tires on your car before leaving.

The scary part about slippery ice conditions is that by the time you find yourself in this slick, and sometimes-uncontrollable driving situation, it's already too late to do anything about it. Though hopefully, and with a little bit of luck, you'll already have at least *some* warning of these icy road conditions up ahead so you're not uncontrollably sliding off the side of the road by the time *you do* realize just how dangerous the driving conditions have become. However, so long as you are still on the road, and if this *is* the case, you have two options: either pull off the road and wait for the ice to melt (not always an option); or you have to push through it with *extreme* caution.

Road Warrior Story - One of the *very worst* icy driving conditions I've ever had to face was during the Winter of 2000. It was late at night and the Winter of 2000 had *already been* a petrifying driving season as it was, but this particular 5-mile stretch of freeway was *the worst ice condition* I'd ever seen or experience before, or since.

I had just left the Tri-Cities area in Washington heading south toward the Oregon boarder when I noticed ALL of the traffic up ahead was driving EXTREMELY slowly. As I started slowing down - it started happening...literally, about every 10-20 feet I drove down the road there were vehicles either flipped upside down or were flipped over on their sides. As I continued on, I started noticing that this strange occurrence of cars and trucks being "flipped over" was happening all along both sides of the freeway – all the way down this particular stretch of the road.

The reality of what I was driving into "sunk in" just about the time I saw a large 20-foot moving truck flipped completely upside down and lying in the ditch on its topside. Now *I knew* it was terrifyingly *slick* on the road!

As I started feeling my tires slipping and sliding a bit on the road, I slowed down in awe of the outrageous number of cars, SUVs, and trucks (large and small – 2-wheel drive and 4-wheel drive) flipped over on both sides of the road. This entire experience became surreal as I looked down at my speedometer and realized I was now only driving about 5 miles an hour through this disaster - and my tires were *still* slipping and sliding all over the place. As this new reality set in, it left me feeling petrified that my little car would soon become the next to join the droves of other wrecked vehicles lining the freeway's ditches all along both sides of the road.

The real problems began when I finally caught up with the crowd of drivers still trying to ease their way forward down the freeway. Now, I'm not sure if it was fortunate or unfortunate that I drove a stick shift (manual transmission) car at the time, but it seemed like every time I even *slightly* let out the clutch while just barely placing the "teensiest" amount of pressure on the accelerator pedal (how you drive a standard transmission car – clutch out, gas in) my car would begin to slide sideways.

I was freaked out to say the least, but mostly because, at this point, I wasn't even driving fast enough for my speedometer to register my driving speed anymore – and yet, here I was spinning out of control! This was insane! It was official! I was panicked!

The Trick to Tip #2

Earlier in this book, I mentioned that "the cell phone" is the Road Warrior Princess' best friend, and this is how *Maintaining a Zen-like State of Mind Technique #2* works. Heaven forbid you find yourself in this type of troublesome driving situation, put that cell phone headset on, and speed dial a friend, a family member, or your significant other, and just have them talk to you. There's something soothing about having somebody you love and who you know loves and cares about your well-being too – having that person just talk to you…about anything. Heck! They can even be saying "peas and carrots" over and over and it still works…because the point is that it's just comforting knowing that you're never alone during times like this – *and this is the trick to this tip!* Reaching out to a loved one will calm you down so you can get through this sort of tough driving situation so long as you have your cell phone already charging with the headset plugged in and readily available for you to use it at a moment's notice. Namely, utilizing your "network" of loved ones in times of nervousness can help you keep your mind focused on getting yourself through the situation *safely*, while inhibiting your mind from going stir-crazy with sidetracking thoughts like, "Geezes, there's another flipped over truck! Oh my gosh! I'm gonna die! I'm gonna die! I'm gonna slide off this road and die!"

Road Warrior Tip: Now, for as much as I had to deal with my own fears during this one very scary night, the other trick in these types of situations is to reach out to whomever you can find to help you put these types of frantic thoughts racing in your mind to rest. More important, you must keep your conviction that you're not going to die because as a Strong Road Warrior Princess, you're not - Not if you maintain your Zen-like state of mind!

As a Road Warrior Princess, it is up to *you* to keep yourself calm, cool, collected, aware of your surroundings, and completely in control of your Road Warrior Adventure! Yes, even under these types of crazy situations – reaching out for help is never without merit!

Peace of Mind Just in the Nick of Time

A Road Warrior Princess KNOWS who the levelheaded and calming people are in her life, so USE THEM to keep you calm when you find yourself in a situation where you're having a hard time keeping your own mind and emotions under control during scary driving situations!

Road Warrior Story Continues - In this particular situation, I used my sister's calming nature to keep me grounded, centered, and clear of mind while I drove through this insanity of flipped over and spinning out of control cars, trucks, and SUVs all the way down that terrifying 5-mile stretch of freeway – and truly, my big sister is great! I think that is why those of us fortunate enough to have an older sibling are sometimes just "a little more daring" in life; we know we can always call *Big Sis'* if we ever need any help! And since I knew this to be the case – my big sister is the person who got my call that night!

The best part about that night *was* my sister's calming nature while I was freaking out – and *that* particular night, I *knew* I was letting my mind run away with me. So, I called her and told her where I was at and what was happening on the road I was traveling. While trying not to completely freak her out, I told her about all of the trucks, cars, SUVs, and moving trucks that were turned upside down and lying on their sides along both sides of the road - How I was going up a hill and I couldn't even touch the gas pedal without the rear of my car trying to slide out from behind me - and when I said, "just talk to me so I can get through this without freaking out"…she talked to me.

About a half an hour later, I was delighted to discover that I had safely arrived at the end of the 5-mile "ice skating rink" in the middle of the freeway. With a sigh of relief, I thanked my sister for keeping me calm and was ready to get safely back on my way down the Open Road!

The moral of this story is that even though you might be a Mighty Road Warrior Princess braving an Open Road Adventure alone, in this day and age, you don't ever have to be *truly alone*, even when you might feel that way. Reach out for a calming voice if you need one and use that cell phone headset so you can keep both hands firmly placed (yet relaxed) on your vehicle's driving controls - and most important - so you *can* keep your eyes on the road! You'll get through it safely!

Maintain a Zen-like State of Mind Technique #3 - Now sometimes you can't get a cell phone signal, or you have found yourself in a situation that is so extensive that you can't possibly stay on the phone *that* long. Maybe you're driving through the Rocky Mountains, or perhaps you're in the middle of the Badlands, where cell phone signals tend to crackle or disconnect all the time; or maybe you're driving through a thunder and lightning storm that is *so bad*, you're afraid to have ANY electrical signals grounding near your head!

In this case, you have officially arrived at the truest "test of will" moment in your Road Warrior Princess Adventures! Congratulations! Nothing will ever test your will to survive, your personal mental strength, your faith and trust in yourself, and your courage, so much as a road trip!

I think that's what I love the most about a good road trip – It is only when out on the Great Open Road alone that you can reveal to yourself who you really are without your friends, family members, significant other, employers, associates, co-workers, and every other person in your life who tends to extend their opinions about you, which usually wind up distorting your own interpretation of your true self to yourself, that you can truly find *your own* inner strengths. Yes, it is out on the Open Road that you will discover your true self!

In order to keep yourself calm in these situations, a True Road Warrior Princess KNOWS her car like she knows her own body. More important, a Road Warrior Princess acknowledges the fact that she knows this. She knows that she understands her own self. She knows that she *will* get herself, "the valuable cargo", delivered safely to her destination.

Road Warrior Story - I remember one time I was driving through a vicious storm up in the mountains. It was windy and raining and the rain was coming down so heavy it looked more like somebody just turned on a garden hose and pushed it right up next to my front windshield more than a mere trickling rainstorm. That was the first major problem.

The second major problem during this experience was that my windows were fogging up faster than the air conditioner and windshield defroster could work. It felt as though my entire world had just jumped into slow motion and the entire experience was starting to suddenly feel very surreal - even the windshield wipers seemed to be moving slower than usual, and they were turned on *Extra Fast* mode!

It was a weird night in that storm, but I was in it. I couldn't see far enough to safely pull off the road because I was in the middle lane on the freeway, and sadly, I knew that I couldn't possibly get over to the side of the road without potentially hitting another car to the rear or side of me. The rain had become so blinding at this point that I just couldn't see any of the cars that had previously been driving near me anymore.

So instead, I "hunkered down" and stood my ground against Mother Nature's fury. I was in this mess and it was my job to make sure I made it safely to my destination. It was just the car, the road, the storm - and lil' ol' me. At this point, I started singing to myself at the top of my lungs, "I will survive"! What a great way to boost your morale and calm your fears of the "what-ifs"!

When faced with such a nerve-racking experience, it is at this point that you want to distract yourself from your fears, in this case I started singing an uplifting self-empowering song, but sometimes just a few little breathing or subtle relaxation exercises can *calm your fears right back down* and put them back in their proper place and perspective again – Which is *out of your head*!

If you find yourself feeling stressed out, tense, or overly nervous behind the wheel of your car - Take a long deep breath, and visualize the oxygen molecules from each calming deep breath penetrating and breaking up the tension in your muscles. Whether it's a cramp in your hand, tension in your shoulders or neck, or jittery muscles in your legs and knees, this technique will usually help you "ground" yourself so you can focus on the driving situation at hand again.

As you begin to relax, notice how your torso and body finally start to ease back into your seat again so that you are now sitting in a more collectively controlled driving position.

Not Allowing Your Tension to Get the Better of You…

This leads me to another big problem I've noticed that many of us experience when we become *too tense* about our driving situation - *We have a tendency to lean in closer to the steering wheel when we get nervous.* DO NOT allow yourself to get too comfy in that "leaning in toward the steering wheel and windshield" driving position! The closer you lean in toward the controls on the front of your car, the more difficult it is for your body to execute short reaction time movements in order to control your vehicle under extreme driving conditions. Relax back into your seat, keep your arms and wrists loose with a firm, yet gentle grip on your steering wheel, and know that YOU CAN get yourself through any situation that the Mighty Open Road intends to throw your way! You are a Road Warrior Princess!

Maintain a Zen-like State of Mind Technique #4 - So this begs the question: What-if you just *really* can't get yourself through this insane driving condition safely? *Not because you feel that **you** are the one who isn't in control of your own car.* It is because you feel as though the situation on the road has now become so chaotic and out of control that it now feels as though *everybody else* can no longer control his or her vehicle - and you have now become scared to death of getting hit by another vehicle on the road.

Road Warrior Story - This was the very type of situation I once encountered in Virginia. I was cruising down the freeway, and sure, it was a little rainy outside, but it wasn't *by any stretch of the imagination* the worst driving condition I had ever driven through. As a matter of fact, it was pretty tame comparatively, but for some reason, the "vibe" (yes, it was that "intuition" thing again) kept yelling at me to get off the freeway!

The freeway was twisting and turning up, around, through, and over "mini-mountain" ranges (as I like to call them), but for some reason the rain just stuck to the road like little droves of flood rails or something. Once the wind began to pick up, the next thing I knew, "hydroplaning in a car" was quickly becoming the new "sporting event" on that particular stretch of freeway that day. Trucks, cars, SUVs, and 18-wheelers alike were hydroplaning and fishtailing all over the road!

As I continued on, the rain started coming down harder and the wind blew us from side to side with more of its vicious fury – and just as the truck next to me with recreational vehicles on it started losing control of its trailer, I noticed a sign to pull off the freeway. That was it! My intuition was SCREAMING at me at this point, so I didn't take extra time to ask questions in my head or second-guess what I was feeling - I just pulled off the road and turned into this little town with a diner. I sat in that diner drinking coffee and eating food (I really shouldn't have been eating) while waiting for the storm to finally pass. After about 3 hours, I was full, tired of waiting, and the storm had finally calmed down enough that it now felt *safe* to get back on the road again.

Just as I was getting back up to speed on the freeway, I had to start slowing back down again. Then I sat in a traffic jam for about an hour. Low and behold, my intuition had been screaming at me for a reason. As I looked further down the road to see what the holdup was on the freeway, there up ahead was one of the trucks that had been driving near me not even 3 hours or so ago. Now it was destroyed and lying on its side on the road up ahead. As I slowly drove closer to the truck, I began to discover just how serious of an accident there had been on the freeway, and for as much as I wanted to think, "Oh my gosh, I could've been involved in that"; I didn't let myself. Instead, I just thanked myself for trusting myself enough to know *when* to get off the road instead of pushing on, in spite of my other feelings about the situation, or second-guessing my inner voice (intuition) about the severity of the situation I had experienced.

The reality is, weird and chaotic situations do happen when you are out on the Open Road! A Great Road Warrior Princess knows when to push through a tough or scary driving situation and when to back off for her own safety. After all, your safety is priority number one when it comes to braving the adventures of the Open Road! Think about it this way: If you let something happen to you, who is going to drive the car?

As a Road Warrior Princess, it is ALWAYS OKAY to pull off the road if you feel you need to pull off in order to avoid danger! This is *very* important to remember! There is nothing wrong with delaying your plans, getting there a little late, or not showing up anywhere even remotely close to "on time" if it is in the interest of your own safety. Besides, not getting hurt during your Road Warrior Adventure is always the best way to *Maintain a Zen-like State of Mind* the next time you get behind the wheel!

Simple Rule 10

Long Drives...

How Does A Road Warrior Princess

Keep Herself Awake?

Rule #10 – Long Drives - How Does a Road Warrior Princess Keep Herself Awake?

Sometimes you will find yourself in a driving situation where you either one, just really *want* to get a little further down the road, or two, you just really *need* to get a little further down the road before you can rest. So how do you keep yourself awake?

Aside from the obvious solutions of cranking up the music really loud, turning on the air conditioner, or rolling down the window to let the wind keep you awake; here are a few other techniques I've found helpful:

Keeping Awake Solution #1 - Remember your favorite traveling hat to keep the light out of your eyes when you're relaxing in a rest area? This is a great resource to use when trying to get a few extra miles out of yourself too! This solution basically falls under the same principles as when you leave the light on in the living room at night so you won't allow yourself to fall sleep until you get up to go turn it off (such as when you're waiting for a certain phone call or for your kids to get home from a party).

The solution is to put your hat on crooked or sideways on your head, then don't let yourself adjust it to fit comfortably on your head again until you reach those extra few miles you needed to drive. This solution works so well because having your hat on your head in an unnatural position will *annoy you* until you reach your destination and because you're annoyed – you will *also* be awake, NOT ASLEEP behind the wheel of your car! I usually use this technique when it's really late at night and I'm trying to find a good rest area to pull over in, or if I know I only have 30 miles (or less) left to drive until I can check in at one of my favorite "Mini-Hotels" in the next town.

Keeping Awake Solution #2 - Most of the time, our eyes become weary and tired from driving long distances because our eyes get dryer after long non-stop hours of staring at never-ending stretches of paved road. A drop or two of saline or eye drops solution can refresh your eyes and help you get at least another 30 to 50 miles (usually) out of yourself. Keeping a small bottle of saline or eye drops solution in your glove box or in the armrest center console of your Road Warrior Vehicle can easily help you get those few extra miles.

Keeping Awake Solution #3 - Singing! Be proactive while you're driving! If you're sitting behind the wheel with your thoughts, driving idly down the road, tuning out the music, and then suddenly find yourself falling into a transient state of mind or feeling as though you are rapidly becoming a zombie behind the wheel of your car – SING as LOUD as you can!

Singing is an amazing way to rejuvenate yourself! The vibrations from your vocal cords send an infinite and revitalizing boost of energy throughout your entire being when you sing! If you're really tired and you're straining to make those last few miles - sing whatever you're feeling as loud as you can with enthusiasm, passion, and gusto! Singing with *emotion* can usually get you at least another good 10-30 miles down the road – or as far as you can stand listening to yourself singing, anyway!

Simple Rule 11

The Journey...

Knowing The Path

Is Like Knowing Yourself.

Rule #11 - The Journey – Knowing the Path is Like Knowing Yourself

Getting to know yourself, understanding yourself, and learning to appreciate your own infinite wisdom, power, and abilities *are* the Journey of the Road Warrior Princess!

A Road Warrior Adventure is as much about getting to know yourself, as it is about getting to know new people, new places, and new experiences. It's like any other great adventure or challenge in life; it is about what you learn about YOU as you follow the road, determine your own course, and navigate that course - ultimately leading to your safe arrival at your new destination wiser and more confident than you were when you first began your journey.

The Inspiration…

As in life, all too often, the greatest adventures and personal growth experiences are neglected, passed up, dismissed, and regarded as "yeah, that'd be nice, BUT…" because we do not feel prepared to take on whatever challenges we may encounter along the way.

This book is your toolbox - It is your survival guide - It is your security blanket. It is all of these things so that you too, *as a strong powerful woman with the mind, attitude, aptitude, intellect, and ability to determine your own course, to chart your own course, and as one who possesses the necessary confidence to safely navigate your own course* CAN explore and embrace these great adventures in hopes that you may better know yourself in this life while embarking upon the many adventures the Open Road has to offer you!

The Challenge…

As with all things in life, you will either read this book and decide to follow your desires to explore the unknown terrains of the land, and thus further explore yourself - or you will submit to your fears and remain silently at home awaiting *someone else* to take you by the hand to show you and to tell you what to do with your life. Whatever you decide after reading this book, know that only *you* can know what is right for you, as in life, as in…when exploring the great adventures of the Open Road!

Should you accept your divine invitation to explore the unknown, to challenge your own unique abilities to take care of yourself, to follow your intuition, and to allow your spirit to be free - You may find that the Road Warrior Princess is not just a woman who knows how to take care of herself out on the Open Road, but that the Road Warrior Princess is the strong, powerful, self-directed woman in all of us.

This book was written with many women in mind; some of who are friends, family members, or acquaintances, and some who are simply women I've met in passing along my journeys. These women inspired me to write this book because all too often I have listened to too many women who are heavy of heart because they felt burdened by their choices to *not fulfill* their true heart's desires. They did not feel they were brave enough, courageous enough, or adventuresome enough to take care of themselves while exploring The Great Unknown.

Alternatively, many other women claimed they did not have enough money, that nobody would come with them, they worried about what-if they got lost or something bad happened, or they believed that they couldn't leave their jobs for that long…and a plethora of other EXCUSES for why they would not listen to, or downright *refused* to fulfill, their own soul and heart's desires for their lives. They gave me many *excuses* for why they believed settling for never straying too far from home, though it may make them miserable at heart and unfulfilled in soul, was the best course of action through non-action for their lives.

Thus, I have concluded that all of these statements have one thing in common - FEAR! The fear of the unknown is a very powerful and great motivator for *doing nothing* you desire to do with your life. As with life, when you take a step forward to do that "thing" you've never done before without really knowing WHAT you're doing and while feeling unprepared for every possible "what-if" that crosses your mind, of course you will let your fear take control. It is far easier to do nothing because of the "what-ifs" than it is to do something to empower yourself, to take on the challenge, and to defeat the "what-ifs" that hold you back from exploring the true adventures that will help you grow, as a person and as a spiritual being, in this life.

The very fact that you bought this book shows me that you are ready to challenge the "what-ifs" and the fears that hold you back from exploring the Open Road. Thus, you are now ready to *challenge* those fears that hold *you* back from exploring and empowering yourself so that you may now become an even stronger woman who lives her life by revealing her true potential.

Fears Addressed...

Before concluding this book, I would like to challenge some of the most common "what-ifs", "but, I could never's", and fears I hear from many women so that you too may start coming up with questions to challenge your own "what-ifs" and fears about exploring the unknown adventures of your own soul and heart's desires:

Fear of the "What-ifs"

Fear #1 - *"What-if"* I'm not Brave, Courageous, or Adventuresome Enough to Take a Road Trip by Myself?

Challenge: What are "Bravery", "Courage", and an "Adventuresome" Spirit?

Bravery is nothing more than having the ability to do what needs to be done when it needs to be done. Alternatively, our expert, the good ol' English Dictionary likes to define bravery as, "Having or displaying courage. To face or endure courageously."

This begs the question: What is "Courage"?

Courage is nothing more than confidence in your own ability to do what needs to be done and that confidence is built through experience.

Of course, if we want to consult our expert again, the English Dictionary, courage is "the ability to face danger without fear."

So, essentially having enough bravery and courage to follow your heart's desires will require that you possess the ability to do what needs to be done when it needs to be done, or according to the English Dictionary, you will need to possess the ability "to have or display" "the ability to face danger" without being so afraid that you do nothing at all.

So, I ask you: Have you been "Brave" and "Courageous" before?

- Have you ever removed a spider from your home?
- Have you ever changed a diaper?
- Have you ever gotten into your car and navigated yourself through 5 o'clock traffic just to get that last ingredient for tonight's dinner recipe at the grocery store?
- Have you ever given childbirth?
- Have you ever cooked over an open flame (even on a gas stove) without knowing *exactly* what that flame may or may not do?
- Have you ever moved to a new town without already knowing somebody who lives there *before* moving?
- Have you ever accepted an invitation to attend an event where you only knew one person or possibly nobody at the event before arriving at the event?
- Have you ever done anything outside of the first home you can ever remember living in during your lifetime?

If the answer is yes to ANY one of these questions, then you have demonstrated that *you do possess bravery and courage* because all of these situations present an element of danger, in one form or another, yet you got through them just fine (hopefully). Not to mention, some of these situations, in your mind, may not even be viewed as something you'd think of as "dangerous", but to others, these very same situations could be considered very frightening.

The point is, we are all very brave and very courageous in our own way, and we all possess the strength to do what needs to be done in the face of danger…and you possess courage and bravery too!

So now that we know you are in fact brave and courageous enough to follow your heart and soul's desires, the questions remain: What is *adventuresome* - and are you adventuresome enough to follow your heart and soul's desires to get out there and explore the Open Road? Let's see...

What is "Adventuresome"?

By definition, "Adventuresome" means, "A bazaar undertaking; an unusual and suspenseful experience; to take risks; to dare."

Now, you're probably wondering why I'm using the dictionary to define these characteristics. The answer is simple, because although I can tell you what *I think*, the real question is whether or not *your* definition of these terms (and fears) are based in reality; hence, the good ol' English Dictionary will act as our basis for reality when defining what our fears are really all about.

So this begs the question, according to the strictest definition: Are you adventuresome? Do you take on bazaar, unusual, or suspenseful experiences? Do you take risks, or *dare* to do *anything* in your life?

To help you find out if you are "Adventuresome", let's answer a few more questions:

- Have you ever flown in an airplane?
- Have you ever driven a car?
- Have you ever taken an over-the-counter drug before reading the full literature outlining every single last one of its possible side effects?
- Have you ever crossed the street outside of the crosswalk lines?
- Have you ever gone shopping amongst the mobs of people during the holiday season at your local shopping mall?
- Have you ever sung in the shower?
- Have you ever been to a college or neighborhood party where somebody got drunk?
- Have you ever had a child?
- Have you ever raised a child?
- Have you ever dropped your child off at day care?

- Have you ever been married?
- Have you ever not been married?
- Have you ever been in a romantic relationship?
- Have you ever played basketball?
- Have you ever been snowboarding or snow or water skiing?
- Have you ever opened up your own business?
- Have you ever started a new job when you had no clue about just *what exactly* it was your new employer expected of you?
- Have you ever moved to a new place to live or moved to a new town?
- Have you ever bought a house?
- Have you ever put down a huge deposit on a new apartment?
- Have you ever bought a car?
- Have you ever ridden your bicycle instead of driving?
- Have you ever depended on public transportation instead of buying a car?

If you answered yes to ANY of these questions, then you are guilty of being daring and taking risks! Congratulations! You are an adventuresome soul! You just don't give yourself enough credit, that's all! Furthermore, you're also guilty of taking on bazaar, unusual, and suspenseful experiences (when thought about or viewed according to others who may have never done such things).

Sounds silly, doesn't it?

However, nearly everything we do in life requires us to engage in some form of adventure because unless we can see further down the timeline of life than everybody else, none of us really know what will happen *next* in our lives; we just think we have a good idea of what will happen next. It's the same thing when you go on a road trip by yourself.

Now that we know *you really are* brave enough, courageous enough, and adventuresome enough to be a Road Warrior Princess, let's explore the other excuses and fears that can hold you back.

Fear #2 - *"What-if"* I Don't Have Enough Money?

This is a great *excuse*, especially considering the state of the U.S. economy during the writing of this book. "I don't have enough money for a Road Warrior Adventure" is extremely justifiable considering the job loss rate, the fact that most households are living paycheck to paycheck, and the fact that most other things like food, shelter, and clothing tend to take priority over embarking upon a "frivolous" Road Warrior Adventure. Of course! You can't afford a Road Warrior Adventure! Right?

Wrong!

You need to ask yourself one question: What are you doing right now that is so incredibly rewarding and fulfilling that you couldn't possibly afford to further your growth as a spiritual being in this life by going on a Road Warrior Adventure out on the Open Road?

This is a question you MUST ask yourself…because if you can't answer this question honestly, then you must consider the fact that maybe you *do* need to get out there on the Open Road and give yourself permission to better understand yourself. The benefit being, that once you return to your home and family or friends, you will have the confidence to put aside your fears in other areas of your life too. Open Road Adventures aren't just about traveling. They're about building the confidence necessary so that *you can do* what you want to do while KNOWING that YOU CAN DO what you want to do with your life - and that YOU CAN FULFILL your true desires and goals for this life without the insecurities (fears) of the "what-ifs" or "but, I could never's" in life holding you back.

Sample Self-imposed Restrictive Thoughts

- ***Are you a single working mom*** who wishes you could start your own business, but won't do it because you know that you *can't afford* to have a month go by without a steady paycheck or health insurance – and now you feel trapped by the expectations you place on yourself because you have a child or children to raise?

- *Are you an artist stuck* in an unfulfilling job with good pay and feel as though you *could never* allow yourself to take a pay cut as drastic as that of a "starving artist" while you pursue your true heart and soul's desires of becoming a great artist?

- *Are you a working mom* who only ever wanted to be a stay-at-home mom but your family *can't afford* to give up your income so you can stay at home with your children?

These are just a few examples of the "but, I could never's" that hold us back from fulfilling our true destinies in life. The best part about the Open Road is that it is "out there" that you will not only find yourself, but you will oftentimes find your answers for how to conquer your other fears that are holding you back in this life, as well.

If the Open Road calls to you, make it a priority! We cover the cost of food because it is a priority – Eatable food is an essential part of our survival because without nourishment for our bodies we will die. The same goes for *food for your soul*. If you have chosen to starve your soul because of "but, I could never" financial excuses then you allow your soul to gradually die. If you do not want to become, or desire to no longer be one of those hollow shelled people we so often see in this world; nourish your soul. Make freeing your being and becoming aware of yourself a priority. More important, budget the Open Road the same way you would budget for groceries.

A Road Warrior Adventure does NOT have to be an expensive endeavor, but it does have to happen in order for you to free yourself enough to find yourself again.

Tips for Financing Your Road Warrior Adventures…

So now that your Road Warrior Adventure is a priority in the family budget, how do you find the money for it in the midst of an over-strapped budget?

I'm not a financial advisor, but the following are a few tips, tricks, and good solid advice that have always helped me find the money to embark on a new adventure whenever I've felt the need to embrace the Open Road the most!

All of the following tips fall under one basic philosophy: Find the "little treats" in your budget and then make the "treat" your road trip.

So what the heck does *that* mean?

Road Trip Financing Tip #1 – Have you ever listened to a *really good* sales pitch? A good sales person can always help you discover just about any amount of money within your monthly budget necessary to purchase their products or services while compelling you to make a purchase so that you now somehow *miraculously* "think" you can afford it and will say "yes" to buying it from them, right then and there - *that very minute*. More important, if what they are selling is already a product or service that you really need or want, say a new shirt, a new couch, a new television, a new stereo, or whatever it is they are trying to sell you - *You will "make" your budget work yourself* so *you can* afford the item that they are selling.

Think about the last big purchase you made; maybe it was a new car, new furniture, a deposit for a new apartment or house, or possibly a new computer? You didn't think you had the money at first, but then you started to REALLY want that "new thing" - and POOF! Just like magic, you found a way to pay for it! Budgeting for a road trip works much the same way.

If you really want the opportunity to be free, to get to know yourself better, to explore the Open Road, to take on the challenge of a new adventure - *You will find the money to pay for your adventure*. By the very nature of our survival instincts, this is what we do, as a people. We find something we want or think we need - and then we come up with a way to get it! Someway - somehow - it just always magically happens. This is the foundation principle behind tip number one...*Believe* you need it and budgeting solutions for how to come up with the funds necessary for your Road Warrior Adventures will appear before you! Just like magic! (Though, most likely, your budgeting solutions will *appear to your mind* through more practical and legal means!)

Road Trip Financing Tip #2 – Figure out where you're spending money on those "little treats" in your budget and then make your Road Warrior Adventure that "One Big Treat" that you are accommodating for in your monthly budgeting, instead of all the other "little treats".

When I talk about "treats", these expenditures can be anything: It could be going to your favorite coffee shop and buying a $5 cup of coffee each morning or it could be spending $10 on lunch every day. The fact is, when you add up *how much money* you spend on these "little treats" (and all those other "little things" that make you feel as though you have no idea where the money goes at the end of each month) – and once calculated; it's easy to see how all of those "little" price tags (expenditures) added together are actually the money that *could* go toward funding your road trip instead. This strategy works great for any larger monetary goals you may have and is especially useful for Road Warrior Adventure financing!

Road Warrior Story - I once showed this simple method to a friend of mine who was struggling a bit each month to cover her bills because she claimed she never had any money and she was tired of living paycheck to paycheck. After discussing her finances with her, I showed her how to use Tip #2 to better utilize her money.

I explained to her that if she just paid the basic bills on a pro-rated time table (according to her pay schedule and the deadlines of when her bills were due) and then she stashed away *some* of her "where did it go?" money, even if it was just stored in an envelope, a tin can, or a glass jelly jar, *before* going out and spending *any* of her leftover money after paying her bills each month – *And* if she stashed away some of this extra cash *before* spending so much as a nickel of each paycheck on frivolous things, such as a candy bar, a soda, a coffee, or a $10 sandwich - Then she would have extra cash sitting around all the time and would never have to worry about "never having enough" again.

After showing her how Tip #2 works, one day she decided to sit down and take my advice. She sat down with a calculator and figured out just *exactly* how much money she would have after 3 months of using this method if she diverted her "where did it go?" money that was being spent on "little treats" into a tin can instead of spending it. At least for a while, anyway - because none of us want to live without those "little treats" forever! True to the method, she realized she would have approximately $2,300 USD in her tin can after nearly 3 ½ months worth of paychecks if she were to keep just a little closer eye on *where* her money went. Wow! With that kind of extra cash lying around, a Road Warrior Princess could afford for a pretty nice Road Warrior Adventure!

The thing is, at the time she was figuring out how to no longer live so "paycheck to paycheck" my friend wasn't making A LOT of money, at least not so much as what one would imagine it might take to save a little over two grand in 3 ½ months. She was working as a customer service representative and making an average income for that position. Yet, even as an average income working American, she discovered that if she would just watch *where* her money goes every paycheck and if she had *just a little more self-directed discipline* with her spending, she'd have a lot more money than she thought she had. After all, it's not how much we make that matters most; it's how much we keep that determines our joy of experiences in this life!

Now I'm not here to write a book on personal finances, that's an entirely separate book and there are literally thousands of books on this very topic at any given book store or online. The point is, if you *really do want the opportunity to go on a Road Warrior Adventure*, chances are – you do have the money to do it! However, until you decide that "being able to embrace the Open Road whenever you want" *is* something that you feel is important for you to have as an option *in* your life, you will never make the proper allowances for these Road Warrior Adventures in your financial budget. So, delete the "little treats" and use the extra cashola to finance your Open Road Adventures!

This brings us to…

Road Trip Financing Tip #3 - Making yourself a priority in your budget is imperative for the Road Warrior Princess! Over the years, I have read a great many inspirational and financial books that all focus on the philosophy of paying *yourself* first! The goal of the Road Warrior Princess is to make sure she not only pays herself first in monetary means, but that she also pays herself first when it comes to those things that money cannot necessarily "buy". Now when I say the things that money cannot buy, yes, money contributes, but you can't just go to the store and go pick yourself up one, at least not just yet; these are things that must be "lived" in order to acquire and appreciate their *true* intrinsic value.

The things that money cannot buy are those "things", such as experiences that truly challenge you - Experiences that will test your own unique abilities - Experiences that will show you who *you* really are to *yourself* without outside influences skewing the reality of who you are to them, or should be, to yourself - Experiences that allow for the opportunities to know yourself and to be in touch with yourself – Most important, experiences that will guide you to listen to and to know your own heart's desires louder and with more clarity than ever before! Those "things" that money cannot necessarily buy are experiences that *afford for you* to live a life that can better enable *you* to discover your own ways of accomplishing the things you aspire to accomplish in this world.

For the Road Warrior Princess, this is the purpose of paying yourself first. Make a commitment to paying yourself first in both monetary and non-monetary means and your experiences out on the Open Road can allow you to find your way so that you may continue to make these "things" possible in your own life, which in turn, can also help you figure out new ways to help yourself financially too.

Fear #3 - *"What-if"* Nobody Will Come With Me?

This is one of the biggest fears I hear from women about why they won't go on a road trip, or any vacation for that matter, by themselves. They are afraid to be alone.

As human beings, we love to be around people. We love to feel like we belong, and to feel as though we are members of a group of people that will love us and will be there for us throughout our journey called "Life", no matter what happens. This is perfectly normal.

The only problem is that if you allow yourself to be defined by your associations, then do you ever really know who *you* are or what *you* think about *your* own life? Do you really know *your own* strengths? Do you really know how much *you* can handle, or how well *you* can solve the various types of problems that arise when on *your own*? Do *you* truly know *yourself*, or do you just think you do?

A Road Warrior Princess knows herself so well that she knows that it doesn't matter if other people won't go on a road trip with her because a Road Warrior Princess KNOWS that she is just as much at ease when being with herself as her only company as she is with being around others whom she loves and trusts.

Do not allow this excuse to hold you back! If you aren't comfortable being by yourself and being in your own company for extended periods of time, such as on a road trip, then maybe this is a sign that you really *do* need to get to know your own best friend again, and that best friend is you! Go on the road trip!

Fear #4 - *"What-if"* I Get Lost?

Remember when you were a little kid and your parents use to tell you to "Stick close by! Don't get lost!" This type of reinforcement to "Not Get Lost" while growing up, has conditioned us to fear the thought of *ever* getting lost. Thus, getting lost is another great fear…but, what *is* getting lost?

Getting lost is nothing more than an unplanned route or detour to your destination. HOWEVER, when thought about a different way, sometimes when we are following the incorrect path to our destination, we must allow ourselves to become lost in order to find our true destination, or destiny if you will. So do not think of getting lost as being a negative thing - Getting lost can oftentimes be the best experience, or gift from the Universe, you can ever give yourself permission to experience in this life!

Sometimes, You Just Have to "Get Lost" to Find Your Way Back…

To demonstrate this point, I'd like to tell you about a recent "getting lost" experience I encountered not too long ago:

Road Warrior Story - It was a hot humid day and I was to attend a seminar at a hotel in a plaza area that I *thought* I knew well. I *thought* I knew exactly where I was suppose to go; I *thought* I knew what roads would take me there; and I *thought* I knew exactly how much time it would take for me to get there from my home.

Just to be on the safe side, I printed up driving directions to my destination off of an Internet website, because although my mind told me I knew exactly where I was going, something deep down inside of me just didn't *believe* I knew where I was going. As it turned out, my intuition was smarter than my conscious memory and the road map I printed off the Internet, combined.

As I drove to my destination, the hotel, I followed the directions I printed and followed my conscious mind's recollection of where this hotel was located. After circling the same roads over and over, I concluded, I was indeed *lost* and pulled into a retail store parking lot to call the service for the seminar in an attempt to receive better driving directions.

Unfortunately, the person on the other end of the phone line was about as good at giving me *helpful* driving directions as the squirrel noshing on a nut next to the side of my car because this individual couldn't give me driving directions either!

Next, I called the hotel, and they couldn't give me useful directions from where I was now located. So, after many failed attempts of searching for help, I just started driving and decided maybe *getting lost* and allowing my intuition (also most notably referred to as the "Super-Subconscious Mind" by various groups of psychologists and spiritualists) to guide me was the best course of action. After all, the map, the seminar hotline, the hotel employee, *and my own conscious memory* had yet to actually help me up to this point.

As I drove around, I turned left and followed that road for a while, then I turned right and I drove past a popular shipping company's customer service building that I knew well. At which point, my first thought was, "Oh man! I really am lost! What the heck am I doing near the shipping customer service building? I'm never going to find this place!" But! I just went with what my intuition was guiding me to do, so I turned another right and a few blocks later, I pulled up to the next streetlight. In all reality, I didn't know why I was allowing myself to get lost; it just felt like the right thing to do.

Road Warrior Tip: When it comes to getting lost and allowing yourself to "just go with the flow" of being lost in order to find your way back again…If it starts feeling as though it's "just the right thing to do", then the only reassurance I can find for allowing *myself* to do such a thing is having faith in knowing that "ALL ROADS CONNECT" (at least in one way or another), so I could never *possibly* be lost forever!

Road Warrior Story Continues - As it turned out, getting lost was the best thing I ever could have done, because there I was, sitting at a light about six cars back from the intersection when I noticed a small sign hidden somewhat behind a tree branch on the left side of the road. The little sign read, "Hotel - Turn Left". Sure, I had to hustle so I could cut my way across two lanes of traffic to get over in the turning lane for the hotel entrance, but by allowing myself to trust my intuition and "just get lost", I allowed myself to find my way back to my final destination in just the nick of time too! Luckily, I entered my seat just as the seminar was about to begin. Had I continued to argue with my memory recollection and the map, or had I continued to get frustrated with what I *thought* was the correct path to my destination, I may never have arrived at my destination in time for the seminar.

The point is, *"don't be afraid of getting lost"* because sometimes getting lost is *the only way* to find the *true course* to your destination in time for the event(s) you are destined to attend in life.

Fear #5 - *"What-if"* Something Happens? Put another way…What-if Something *Bad* Happens to Me?

This is one of our biggest fears. Specifically, this is one of the biggest fears of those being alone. What-if something bad happens to me and nobody is there to help me? It's true, the world is more overpopulated than ever before, so truly being alone is unlikely; however, the world is also more impersonal than ever before too. Hence, even if you aren't physically alone, you may still feel alone. Welcome to the double edge sword of the new millennium – Being alone in a crowded world!

The best way to deal with this fear is to think of the very worst thing that could possibly happen, and I do mean, think of *the very worst* possible thing that could happen to you. What is your greatest fear about traveling the Open Road alone? Is it getting in a car accident, or possibly getting your purse stolen, or maybe having a strange person attack you outside a restroom, or possibly, it's somebody breaking into your car, or having your car breakdown on the side of the road? Right now, I want you to pick the VERY WORST thing that could possibly happen to you when you are out on the Open Road. I want you to visualize that one thing that always comes to mind every time you think "but what-if *something* happened?" - and I want you to visualize all of the not so pleasant details your mind/fear can come up with concerning this particular scenario.

Now that you have that terrible "what-if *something* happens" scenario in your head, I want you to *rewrite* the script in your mind. While you're sitting here in your safe environment reading this book, I want you to think of, and visualize in your mind's eye what it would take for you to see this bad situation turn into a not so bad situation, because in the end, you wind up safe and happily back on your way.

Sample Empowering "Yourself" Instead of "Your Fear" Scenarios

IF in your fear scenario you see yourself winding up stranded on the side of a freeway with a flat tire, ***THEN*** visualize yourself discovering the nail in your tire during one of your routine tire checks at the gas station followed by visualizing yourself pulling your car into a tire service center, the tire service center technician repairing your tire, and you driving down the freeway again with peace of mind and confidence that the tire will now no longer go flat – Nor will you become stranded on the side of the freeway in your fear scenario because now you have fixed the problem that caused this fear scenario in the first place, *before* it had a chance to disturb your Road Warrior Adventure.

OR,

Using the same fear scenario of being stranded on the side of the road with a flat tire; alternatively, you could visualize that - okay, maybe you *still* wound up with a flat tire on the side of the road, but *now* visualize yourself replacing the flat tire on your car yourself with the spare tire in the trunk of the car.

After visualizing the successful changing of the tire, allow yourself *to feel* that sense of accomplishment that comes with feeling proud of yourself for possessing the "know-how" and the strength to take care of yourself so intelligently during such a potentially negative experience.

Finally, visualize yourself driving down an off-ramp on the freeway, pulling into a nearby tire service center, having the damaged tire repaired or replaced, and then getting back onto the freeway with peace of mind!

These little visualization exercises will help you build the internal strength, a sense of self-awareness, and feelings of accomplishment for having completed a job well done (in your mind) - so you can start having faith within that, given the opportunity in life, *you do* possess the confidence and knowledge necessary to take care of yourself when out on the Open Road alone!

"What-if Something Bad Happens?"

Although the tire scenario is frightening, sometimes our "what-if something happens?" scenarios are far scarier than merely getting a flat tire by the side of the road and not being able to repair it. Sometimes bad things do happen - Things we feel we wouldn't be able to control if it did happen to us, such as being attacked by someone. This is a very large fear among many women. You're not alone! Let me tell you right now - It is okay to have these fears, because that fear is what keeps you safe by keeping you prepared and aware of your surroundings at all times, should something like this ever happen to you. At the same time, these fears need to be addressed if you are to enjoy living your life without living in fear – and for you to be able to to follow your heart's desires for this life without allowing your fears to create and enforce self-restrictions against your own sense of happiness.

Sample Empowering "Yourself" Instead of "Your Bad Fear" Scenarios

So let's address the example of somebody attacking you – let's say this is *your* "something" in the endless list of possible scenarios that could happen when thinking of "what-if something *bad* happens to me?"

In this scenario, as in the previous, I want you to visualize the *very worst* of this scenario that you fear. Maybe somebody is jumping out and attacking you, or forcing you into a car, or whatever your imagination's fear is, visualize this fear scenario in your mind.

Now that you have this image in your mind, I want you to think of the "one thing" that would change how this scenario is playing out in your mind's eye right now:

Maybe you visualize an animated comical twist to the scenario and kick the person attacking you so hard that this person is so shocked and bewildered by what just happened and by your powerful reaction to being attacked by them that they turn around and run away from you! Congratulations! You have escaped the fear scenario victorious!

OR,

Maybe you use a more forceful visualization and you break his nose, or kick him in the shins, run away to your car, and safely drive off without harm or injury.

OR,

Maybe your "one thing" that would make this fear scenario situation better is far more graphic than the scenarios this book can describe.

No matter what you visualize, you have now changed this fear scenario playing out in your mind's eye into a victorious outcome instead of your greatly feared outcome!
  The most important thing to remember when doing these visualization exercises, is that regardless of *what* you visualize to empower yourself to break free of the fear scenario playing out in your mind's eye – always visualize *yourself* doing the "one thing" that would make this situation turn from a bad situation into a not so bad situation – and be graphic! Be detailed! Be over-the-top! Be superhuman if you have to be in your visualization! Just make sure you *see* yourself, in *your* mind's eye, defeating this fear and beating it down until it disappears from your list of inner fears!
  Notice how you feel just visualizing yourself defeating this feared situation. Do you feel victorious, empowered, hopeful, proud, or angry, yet happy? Whatever you are feeling by defeating this feared scenario is okay. Remember it. You ARE NOT your fears! You are bigger and braver, and stronger than your fears, and through visualization, you CAN defeat any fear based in the "but, what-if something happens?" realm of your imagination!

Always Mentally Defeat the Challenges First!

Practice this technique with every "but, what-if something happens?" fear that comes to your mind - and I do mean EVERY SINGLE ONE of them! As you find mental solutions to defeat the fear holding you back by turning these potentially negative situations into positive outcomes in your mind - you may slowly start finding yourself feeling more confident in your own abilities to handle whatever situations may come your way. This is because you have already *visualized* your victory in that given situation in your mind - and doing it in your mind's eye *is* the key, and half the battle to accomplishing *anything* in real life!

If you can see it and believe it - If you *know* you have a plan and have already *thought* about the "what-ifs" - Then you can feel more confident that *you will be able to handle* the situations that may or may not come your way while exploring the amazing adventures that the Open Road has to offer every Road Warrior Princess who is willing to accept its invitation. This is a mental exercise to help strengthen your willpower and your ability to cope with any situation on or off the Open Road! You can take care of yourself in any situation; you just need to be prepared - and this is just another way the Road Warrior Princess prepares herself. She is mentally prepared!

Fear #6 - *"What-if"* I Have Kids? What Am I Suppose to Do With Them? I Can't Leave!

This is an excellent point! What-if you're not single, not without children: Can you still live the life of a Road Warrior Princess?

You Bet You Can!

Just because you're a mother raising a child or children does *not* mean you have to stop living your life, or that you have to stop pursuing your spiritual growth via the means of Open Road exploration! It just means that *now* you have to lead by example! You are the role model! You are the one making sure your children grow up understanding that they are also unique and powerful beings, just like you! By demonstrating and incorporating the philosophies and the awareness tools of the Road Warrior Princess, you will be an example and a guide when helping your children safely find their own way in the world. After all, you may wind up raising some very adventuresome children. Wouldn't it be nice to know that *you know* that *they know* how to take care of themselves?

However, this begs the question: Do you take the kids with you on *your* Road Warrior Adventures, or do you leave them at home?

Honestly - BOTH!

As a mom, you need some downtime - and you need to give yourself permission to take the time you need to keep your head in check, maintain your focus, and to find *yourself* as much as you need to be a good mother. After all, sometimes this is the *very best way* to keep yourself fully charged to take care of your kids by knowing that *sometimes you just need to take time for you too!*

On the other hand, there is nothing like a family road trip! Bring the kids along, or better yet, start teaching them about the car and then *they* will want to change that flat tire for you if you happen to "get a flat" on your Road Warrior Adventures together! Better yet! Assign the "checking of the tires" tasks to one of the kids and let them learn for themselves how incredibly important it is to always take care of your Road Warrior Vehicle when traveling the Open Road!

Now if you do want to embrace the Open Road on your own, here are a few suggestions:

- Send the kids to summer camp and take a summer Road Warrior Adventure for a couple of weeks on your own.

- Let the kids stay at their grandparent or grandparents' home for a week and now that you know they're in safe hands - Take on the Open Road! Afterwards, you will be calmer and more ready to deal with the little day-to-day details of life that can oftentimes get to the point of driving you crazy!

- If you're divorced, let them stay with dear ol' dad, or their other guardian for a while. However, if that's not an option, see if a sibling or trusted friend would like to watch them for a few days and then go travel the Open Road with gusto!

- If you're not divorced, well, that's why you have a partner in life, right?

Every family has their own situations to deal with and familial structure. The point is to make sure that, as a mom, you now understand that just because you are a mom, this doesn't mean you *have* to let your soul and heart's aspirations to brave the Open Road as a Road Warrior Princess dissipate into thin air "just until the kids are grown up" and out of the house. When you need time to yourself, you need to give yourself permission to take it.

A Road Warrior Princess Mom knows that if she can keep herself balanced, she can be a mom with the peace of mind and the mental and emotional elasticity to always be there for her kids and to calmly deal with whatever mess her children happen to create for her to cleanup! A Road Warrior Princess Mom is the same as any Road Warrior Princess; she is *always prepared* for *whatever* may come her way!

Fear #7 - *"What-if"* I Can't Leave My Job for *Too* Long?

This is a great excuse! I've worked for a few relentless employers before too! My advice for you is this: If you can't even take 24 consecutive hours to yourself, then *you are the one person who needs to take time for yourself the most*! Pen it into your day planner and don't cancel this appointment with yourself!

No Paid Vacation Time? No Problem!

So what-if you are a freelancer, or a woman who works for herself running her own business? I can hear you all right now saying, "I don't *work* for anyone! I set my own hours - I work hard - and I like what I do! I just don't have the time to step away from my work for a road trip."

I can understand these feelings because I have been known to demand 30 hour workdays from myself (yeah, you do the math on that one!) without letting myself stop for time off until I got the job done, or at least until I have met the deadline I needed to meet.

The point is that it is okay to work hard. Work as hard as you want to work, or as hard as you need to work, to accomplish what you need to accomplish in life. Just remember to give yourself a break to avoid burnout. I once had a surfing buddy back in college that lived by one rule of life: "Work hard! Play hard!" This is a great philosophy! I ultimately decided to listen to him after I finally burnt-out because I'd been burning the candle at both ends of the wick (so to speak) for far too long. In order to give 110% at your work, *you must* allow yourself to relax and reconnect with your inner being 110% from time to time too.

This concept is commonly referred to as "balance", "yin-yang", or "Newton's Third Law of Motion" stating, "to every action there is an equal and opposite reaction." Hence, if you are working hard and have no time for *you*, one way or another the Laws of the Universe will eventually demand that your lifestyle pattern become balanced back out with equal downtime to equal uptime. If you're not paying attention, the Universe may just end up shutting down your world *for you* (of which, I can also relate).

My suggestion is that you acknowledge this Simple Universal Law, apply the finance and budgeting tips in this book, and schedule the downtime into your life for *yourself.* This way, you may take the downtime you need to maintain balance in your own life *when you want to take it*, and *not* when you are feeling forced by Universal Laws that *insist* you must take it!

Closing Words

A Road Warrior Princess knows that a True Road Warrior Adventure doesn't always have to be lengthy and extensive. Sometimes it's just a matter of driving to the ocean or the mountains; or a new little town you always wanted to go visit, but have never been able to get around to seeing it; or taking a trip to the Grand Canyon, or any other major tourist attraction you have always wanted to experience, but never found the time. After all, you may only be 4-5 hours away from any number of amazing locations, and yet, maybe you have never just jumped in your Road Warrior Vehicle to go see *any* of them!

I have been all over this country (and a few others too) and the one thing I know to be true is that every state and region has at least *some kind* of tourist attraction. Become a Road Warrior Tourist in your own state for the day and see where the Great Open Road guides you. Live a little! Get to know your state and these experiences just might lead you toward even greater opportunities of venturing out to see *even more* of the fascinating world around you.

The more you know about your world, the more you will discover about yourself and who you are in this world. Never allow yourself to believe that the learning process of self-awareness and self-discovery is over just because you think you already know all that you think you should or will need to know. After all, you are here because you are green and growing!

Learn more, explore more, adventure more, discover more, see more, and give yourself the tools to become more! You are a Great Road Warrior Princess and possess the infinite wisdom and power to become so much more! Follow your heart and soul and discover your true goals for this life. Follow the road and see where it takes you as you embrace both the physical and the spiritual journey of Road Warrior Adventures and Open Road Discovery!

    Now that you have read this book, I hope that you will do what this book encourages you to do - Go find your Road Warrior Vehicle; prepare yourself, both mentally and physically, in knowing your car like you know your own body; and take this book with you once you have committed to overcoming your fears by getting out there on the Open Road and accepting the challenge! Embrace your invitation to explore this great world! You are a Road Warrior Princess!

Simple Rules

for...
The Road Warrior Princess!

Quick Guide Index

Quick Guide Index

3-Point Parking, 88
Accident, 13-14, 36, 49-50, 90-91, 116-117, 124, 129, 151
Accidental Oil Leak, 9-10
Adventuresome, v, x, 138-142, 155
Affirmation, xii
Airbag, 4
Air Conditioner, Air Conditioning, 4-5, 22, 95, 101-104, 127, 133
Air Filter, 34, 78
Alternative Fuel, 81-82
Antifreeze, 11, 25-27, 101-103
Armrest, 12, 48, 134
Auto Parts (Store), 6, 9-10, 28, 32-34, 46, 103, 105
Blanket, 14, 45-46, 60, 137
Blowout, 40, 106-107
Brakes, 4, 28, 36, 83-85, 90, 109, 116-117
Braking, 36, 83-85
Brake Fluid, 28
Bravery, x, 138-142, 154-156

Breakfast, 69
Breakdown, Broke Down, 12, 17, 103, 151
Budget, 17, 67, 77, 80, 99, 144-148, 158
Calm, 86, 106, 121-130, 156-157
Cap, Brake Fluid, 28
Cap, Engine Oil, 24
Cap, Gas, 13
Cap, Radiator, 25-27, 102-103
Cap, Radiator Coolant Reserve Container, 25-27, 102-103
Cap, Steering Fluid, 27-28
Cap, Tire Valve Stem, 30
Cap, Transmission Fluid, 28
Cap, Windshield Wiper (Washer) Fluid Holder, 25
CD Player, 5, 21
Cell Phone, 6, 47-48, 107, 124-126
Challenge, x, xii, 38, 137-139, 145, 147, 154-155, 160
Chart (Your Own Course), 82, 137

Civil Air Patrol Search and Rescue, 17
Cold, 11-15, 25-29, 40, 61-62, 88, 91, 93, 95, 102
Cold Weather, 10-15, 25-29, 40, 61-64, 93, 102
Collapsible Rear Seats, 6-7, 46
Commitment, 148, 160
Condensation, 17-19, 22, 109
Continental Divide, 3, 69
Control, 4-5, 21-22, 29, 47, 53, 59, 82-95, 105, 109, 116, 122-128, 138, 153
Control, Lose (Out Of Control), 90-95, 83, 116, 123-129, 153
Courage, x, 126, 138-142, 160
Crosswind, 96
Cruise Control, Autocruise, 87
Daily Errands, Errands, 29, 88
Defrost, 5, 22, 127
Desert, 10-11, 17, 20, 104
Donut (Spare Tire), 7, 9, 107-108, 152
Drafts, Drafting, 89-95, 116
Driver's License (I.D.), 49-50
Economy Car (Econocar), 3, 80-81
Emergency, viii, 13-14, 49-50, 90, 99, 101, 111
Emergency Car Escape Tool, 13-14
Emergency Fuel Additive, 101
Emergency Fund, 49-50
Emergency Medical Kit, 14
Empower, xii, 7, 59-60, 82, 127, 137-139, 152-155, 159-160

Engine Belts, 79
Engine Power, 89
Environmental Protection Agency (EPA), 83
Essentials, 6, 36, 46, 78, 80, 88, 144
Excuses, 137-158
Exhaust System, 109
Eye Drops, 134
Family, iii, v, 11, 32, 38, 53, 57, 124-126, 138, 143-144, 156
Fear, x, xii, 12, 30-32, 77, 107, 125, 127-128, 138-160
Finance Budgeting, Financing, 144-148, 158
Flat Tire, ix, 29, 105-108, 152-153, 156
Flood, 129
Fluid Line, 23-28
Fog, 4, 21-22, 127
Fog Light, 5, 122-123
Freezing, 6, 10-11, 13, 25-28, 46, 102
Fuel-efficiency, Fuel Economy, 80-88, 95-96
Fuel (Gas) Gauge, 90, 93-94, 99-100
Fuel (Gas) Mileage, 3-4, 40, 77, 79, 83, 91, 100-101
Fuel (Gas) Price, 4, 77
Fuel (Gas) Station, viii, 9, 13, 27-30, 40, 69-74, 81-82, 93-95, 101, 105-106, 109-111, 152
Fuel (Gas) Stop, 95, 101, 106
Fuel Up (Fill Up), 13, 39, 62, 77, 80, 84, 95, 100-101
Garbage Bag, 14-15, 19-20

Global Positioning System (GPS), 11
Glove Box, 9, 12, 30, 48, 134
Green and Growing, 159
Green Automotive, 81-83
Green Light, 85
Greenhouse Effect, 17
Hat, 59-60, 133
Headlight, Headlamp, 32, 41, 93, 95, 116, 122
Headset, 47-48, 124-126
Headwind, 96, 100
Heater, 5, 15-16, 61-62, 104
Heat Wave, 17
High-speed, 4, 110-111
Hitchhikers, 66-67
Hoodie, 61
Horsepower, 3-4
Humid, Humidity, 4, 22, 34, 149
Hybrid, 80-81
Hydration, 17-20
Hydroplaning, 129
Hypothermia, 15-16
Ice, Icy, 10, 13, 16, 108, 123-126
Idle, 61-62, 86, 100
Inspiration, x, 137, 147
Insurance, 99, 143
Intuition, xii, 62, 65-66, 129, 138, 149-150
Jumper Cables, Jump Start, 10
Keys, 3, 61-62
Kids, x, 11, 15, 89, 133, 140-141, 143-144, 149, 155-157
Lodging, 65-69
Lost, x, 73, 138, 149-151
Map, Driving Directions, 11, 47, 62, 87, 149-151
Mechanic, vii, 3, 10, 23, 32, 36-39, 105, 109
Metal Cup, 15-19
Miles per Gallon (MPG), 3-4, 40, 77-96, 100-101
Mini-Hotel, viii, 67-69, 133
Moisture, 18
Money, x, 7, 11-13, 37, 49-50, 69, 86-89, 138, 143-148
Motels, 48, 62, 67-69
Mother Nature, 63-65, 108, 127
Mountain, v-vi, xii, 3, 6, 48, 69, 100, 116, 126-129, 159
MP3, 5, 21, 47-48
Multipurpose Tool, 12-15, 19
Navigate, 5, 94, 137, 140
Newton's Third Law of Motion, 158
Night, 10, 46
Night, Alone/Sleeping, viii, 10, 15-16, 57-70
Night, Driving, xi-xii, 5, 47, 63-66, 73, 93-95, 116, 123-128, 133-134
Night, Gas (Fuel) Stations, viii, 62, 69-70, 73-74, 81-82, 93-95
Night, Keep Warm, 15-16, 61-62
Non-negotiable Features, vii, 3-7, 45-46, 60-61
Oil, Engine Oil Change, 9, 24-25, 30-32, 35, 40-41, 78-79
Oil, Engine Oil Check, 9-10, 23-25, 39

Oil Filter, 78-79
Oil Funnel, 9-10
Oil, Weight, 9
One Stop Shopping, 6-7, 10, 73
Overheating, ix, 12, 27, 101-105
Overnight, 58, 66
Packing, viii, 45-49
Park (Parking), Pull Over, 5, 24, 47, 49, 58-70, 88-89, 105, 109-111, 133, 150
Planning, v, 8, 20, 35, 47, 50, 57, 66, 68-70, 80-82, 88, 96, 101, 106, 130, 149, 154-155, 157
Personal Growth, 137
Powertrain, 83
Power, Power Source Plug, 6, 10, 47-48
Power Steering, 27-28
Radiator, 10, 25-27, 101-104
Radio, 5, 10, 12, 21, 105
Rain, Raining, Rainy, 10, 22, 109, 127-129
Rainstorm, 4, 19, 22, 32, 36, 127
Relaxation, Relax, 60, 68, 121-130, 133, 157
Rest Area, viii, 5, 40, 45, 57-70, 105, 110-111, 133
Revolutions per Minute (RPM), 79-85
Road Advisory, 5
Road Atlas, 11, 47, 62, 87
Road Trip Essentials, 46
Roadside Assistance, 68, 99, 107
Rotors, 36

Safety, v, viii, 4-5, 7, 12, 20, 22, 29, 36-37, 45-50, 57-64, 73, 78, 84, 87, 90-95, 101, 130
Safety Feature, 46, 60, 90, 95
Safety (Location), 73
Safety Rules, vi
Safety Tips, 57
Salting Trucks, 63
Service Center, 9, 24, 27, 29-41, 73, 102-109, 152
Shocks, 36
Side View Mirror(s), 5, 60-61
Simple Survival Kit, vii, 14-20
Sing, 86, 105, 121, 127, 134, 141
Slick, ix, 36, 108, 123-126
Slide, ix, 101, 108, 123-126
Slippery, 101, 108, 124
Slipping Belt, 79
Slow Down, Reduce Speed, 83-87, 94, 105, 109, 116-118, 121-130
Slow Driving, 3, 64, 83-87, 107, 129
Slow Drivers, Slow Traffic, 3, 83-87, 123-124, 127, 129
Snow, Snowy, vi, ix, 63-64, 108
Snowbank, 108
Snowfall, 63-64
Snowplow, 63
Snowstorm, 22, 25, 63-66, 108
Snow Blizzard, 36, 63-66
Snow (Melt), 16
Soil, 17-19
Solar Still, 17-19
Spark Plugs, 79
Speed Limit, 87, 100-101

QUICK GUIDE INDEX

Spiritual, vi, xi, 121, 139, 143-144, 155, 160
Spiritualist, 150
Spiritual Growth, 155
Starvation, 16
Stay Warm, Keeping Warm, 6, 14-16, 61-62
Steering Fluid, 27-28
Steering, Steering Wheel, ix, 21, 27-29, 37, 47, 90-95, 105, 109, 121-122, 128-130, 133-134
Stop, Stopping, 3, 5, 40, 49, 58, 63, 66, 68-69, 83-85, 88, 90-91, 106, 108-109, 111, 116-117
Stoplight, Traffic Light, 84-85, 116
Stop-and-Go Traffic, 83, 85
Stop Sign, 84-85
Stranded, 7, 11, 13, 15-17, 20, 27, 105-108, 152
Strange Noise, 31, 60, 109
Strangers, Strange People, 10, 53, 60, 66-67, 90,151
Strange Situations, 12, 31, 53, 60, 65-67, 108-109, 123, 127, 130
Struts, 36
Sun, 12, 17-20, 36, 48, 65, 95-96, 103-104
Sunscreen, 48
Sunstroke, 12
Surroundings, xii, 57, 66-67, 121, 125, 153
Survival, vi-vii, 7, 9, 14-22, 47, 50, 92-95, 121, 137, 144-145
Survival Instincts, 145
Survival Skills, vi
Survival Technique, 14-20, 92, 121
Survival Tips, 17-18
Survival Tools, vii, 7, 9-20, 95
Suspension, 36
SUV, 46, 80, 88, 117, 124-126, 129
Taillight, 9, 32, 41
Tailpipe, 109
Tailwind, 3, 96
Technician, 9, 31, 35, 37, 41, 105, 109, 152
Temperature, 29, 40, 62, 102
Tense, Tension, 121-130
Terrain, 83, 86, 101, 138
Thermostat, 101-105
Thirsty, 17
Timing Belt, 35-36
Tire Air Pressure, 29-32, 39-41, 77-78, 115
Tire Air Pressure, Checking, 29-32, 39-41, 77-78
Tire Air Pressure Gauge, 9, 29-32
Tire Air Pressure, Pounds (of pressure) per Square Inch (psi), 29-32, 77-78
Tire Chains, 108
Tire Sidewall, 29-32, 39-41, 77-78, 106
Tire, Slow Leak, 29, 106
Tire Traction, ix, 108
Tire Tread, 36, 40, 106, 108
Toll Road, 73
Tools, vii, 3, 7-19, 32-34, 80, 95, 155, 159

Tool Kit, 7-9, 32, 34
Toolbox, 137
Tornado, vi, xi, 5, 36
Tow Truck, 104, 107-108
Traffic, 6, 47, 59, 63, 82-86, 91-92, 100, 106, 109-111, 123, 129, 140, 150
Traffic Violation, 91-92
Transmission, 4, 28, 80-85, 109, 124
Transmission Fluid, 28
Transmission Types, 80-85
Travel Alone, v-vi, viii, xi-xii, 3, 12-13, 21-23, 39, 46, 48, 57-70, 73, 109, 121, 124, 126, 148, 151-153
Travel Coupons, 68
Travel Plaza, 73
Trucks, Tractor-Trailer, ix, xi, 3, 58, 63-64, 69, 90-95, 110, 115-118, 123-126, 129
Truck Driver, Trucker, ix, 58, 64, 69, 90-95, 115-118
Trunk, 6, 9-11, 13-14, 20, 24, 32, 45-46, 101-102, 107-111, 152
Tune-up, 35, 38
Turn Signal, 32, 41
United States Department of Agriculture, 18
U.S. Department of Energy, 82
Vacation, vi, 148, 157
Vegetation, 17-20
Visualize, Visualization, 90, 122, 128, 151-155
Warm Climate, Hot Weather, 4, 11-12, 17, 27, 29, 40, 48, 103-104, 149
Warm Engine, 88

Warm Up Car, 6, 15, 61-62, 88
Water, as Coolant, 27, 102-103
Water, as Windshield Washer (Wiper) Fluid, 11
Water, Drinking Water, Bottle of Water, 5, 10, 16-20, 47, 102
Water, Drips on Wires, 9
Weather Channel, Weather Report, 6, 63
Weather Conditions, 4-8, 10-11, 13, 25-29, 36, 40, 62-63, 69, 95-96, 101-104, 108-109
Weight, Oil, 9
Weight, Vehicle, 80-81, 87-88, 117
Wheel Alignment, 36-37
Willpower, "Test of Will", v-vi, 121, 126, 154-155
Wind, vi, 3, 5, 16, 36, 64, 80-81, 88-89, 93-96, 100, 110, 116, 127, 129, 133
Winding, Winding Road (Curves), xii, 5-6, 27, 48, 116, 121-122, 129
Window, Windshield, 4-5, 9-11, 14, 21-22, 25, 32-34, 48-49, 60-61, 67, 104, 115, 127-128, 133
Windshield Washer (Wiper) Fluid, 10-11, 25
Windshield Wiper, 9-10, 22, 25, 32-34, 127
Winter, 5-6, 8, 10-13, 25-27, 46, 61-62, 65, 69, 93, 102, 108, 123
Wires, 8-9, 79
Wobbling Tire, Wobbling Wheel, 40, 105-107

Simple Rules for…
The Road Warrior Princess

About The Author

Debbie Anderson was born in California and raised in Idaho. She graduated with two degrees: One in Visual Communications and the other in Film and Video Production. Over the course of a decade, Debbie traveled and moved across the country several times in pursuit of exploring the world around her. She now applies and expresses the knowledge she gained from those various journeys through her creative interests, such as informative entertainment media productions and consumer entertainment products. She founded Eminence Enterprises, LLC, an informative entertainment media company, and has served as a guide and video producer for other various How-To and Infotainment Media Companies, such as About.com (a part of The New York Times Company). Currently, Debbie lives in New Jersey and works as a writer, producer, and director in New York City.

Simple Rules for…
The Road Warrior Princess

Reviews: Look At What They're Saying!

"A great source of information to make any woman comfortable to travel on her own. This book contains a wealth of information which neatly slides into your glove compartment. It's good to have it close by because you never know when you just might want to take off and explore a bit!" – *Private Review*

"This book is a useful tool in calming one's own fears of traveling by yourself. When used in conjunction with a little common sense (or...when used in conjunction with other helpful tools and ideas in this book) you should be ready for any situation that could possibly arise." – *Private Review*

"A useful aide to keep by your side when traveling; this book fits nicely in your glove compartment." – *Private Review*

"This book is the ultimate lifeline when traveling. From hotels and car safety to how to finance a trip and get away, even just for a few days, it'll answer your every question." – *Private Review*

To Order More Copies for Your Friends and Family Members, or

To Carry This Book in Your Store – Visit online at:

SimpleRulesOnline.com

Simple Rules...
...for more information!

Visit online at: **SimpleRulesOnline.com**

Made in the USA